ALI AND DAHLIA

by Tariq Jordan

samuelfrench.co.uk

FOR PROFESSIONAL AND AMATEUR PRODUCTION ENQUIRIES

UNITED KINGDOM AND WORLD EXCLUDING NORTH AMERICA
plays@samuelfrench.co.uk
020 7255 4302/01

UNITED STATES AND CANADA
info@samuelfrench.com
020 7255 4302/01

Each title is subject to availability from Samuel French, depending upon country of performance.

Acting Editions

BORN TO PERFORM

Playscripts designed from the ground up to work the way you do in rehearsal, performance and study

---

Larger, clearer text for easier reading

Wider margins for notes

Performance features such as character and props lists, sound and lighting cues, and more

---

+ CHOOSE A SIZE AND STYLE TO SUIT YOU

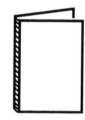

STANDARD EDITION

Our regular paperback book at our regular size

SPIRAL-BOUND EDITION

The same size as the Standard Edition, but with a sturdy, easy-to-fold, easy-to-hold spiral-bound spine

LARGE EDITION

A4 size and spiral bound, with larger text and a blank page for notes opposite every page of text – perfect for technical and directing use

LEARN MORE   **samuelfrench.co.uk/actingeditions**

ABOUT THE AUTHOR

Tariq Jordan is an actor, teacher, and writer based in London. He trained at Webber Douglas Academy of Dramatic Arts and the Royal Central School of Speech and Drama, graduating in 2007. He has worked extensively as a performer on stage and screen.

His TV credits include: *White Girl* by Abi Morgan, *George Gently*, *Spooks*, *Lewis*, *Shameless*, and *Law and Order*.

Theatrical credits include: *Guantanamo* (Tricycle Theatre, New Ambassadors, West End, House of Congress, and House of Commons); *Wah! Wah! Girls* (Sadler's Wells / Kneehigh); *The Bomb* (Tricycle Theatre); Pip in *Great Expectations* (Watford Palace / English Touring Theatre); *This Flesh is Mine*, and *When Nobody Returns* (Border Crossings); *Fragile Land* (Hampstead Theatre).

As a qualified teacher, Tariq has worked extensively with young people in UK state schools and has also taught in the Middle East. His debut play *Ali and Dahlia* was inspired by his experiences working in Palestine as well as having Russian-Jewish and Iraqi-Muslim heritage.

AUTHOR'S NOTE

The original production was performed in the round.

Projected footage was incorporated throughout the piece, and also during scene transitions, to immerse the audience into the locations and time-frames of the play.

The translations have been omitted to accommodate for future productions and castings. The original production contained Palestinian Arabic and Israeli Hebrew dialects.

SETTING

Palestine and Israel: Al-Jalame Prison, a secluded part of the West Bank wall, Qalandia Checkpoint, Jaffa beach, and Gaza's buffer zone.

The play spans from 2002, during the second Intifada and the construction of the West Bank wall, to May 2018 and the opening of the US embassy in Jerusalem.

NOTE ON TEXT

(/)   Denotes an overlapping of dialogue.
(—)   Denotes an interruption.
(...)   Denotes an unspoken continuation of thought or action.

MUSIC USE NOTE

Licensees are solely responsible for obtaining formal written permission from copyright owners to use copyrighted music in the performance of this play and are strongly cautioned to do so. If no such permission is obtained by the licensee, then the licensee must use only original music that the licensee owns and controls. Licensees are solely responsible and liable for all music clearances and shall indemnify the copyright owners of the play(s) and their licensing agent, Samuel French, against any costs, expenses, losses and liabilities arising from the use of music by licensees. Please contact the appropriate music licensing authority in your territory for the rights to any incidental music.

IMPORTANT BILLING AND CREDIT REQUIREMENTS

If you have obtained performance rights to this title, please refer to your licensing agreement for important billing and credit requirements.

CAST

WAJ ALI - ALI
Theatre includes: *LOVE* (NT on tour); *Occupational Hazards* (Hampstead Theatre); *Clothes Swap Theatre Party* (Forward Theatre Project); *The Rest of Your Life, Nahda* (Bush Theatre); *King Lear* (National Theatre).
Film includes: *90 Minutes*; *Good People*; *Red 2*.
Television includes: *Carnival Row* (Amazon); *Mister Winner*; *Witless*; *The Attack*; *Strike: The Silkworm* (BBC); *Stan Lee's Lucky Man* (Sky).

DELI SEGAL - DAHLIA
Deli read English at Robinson College, Cambridge and trained at East 15 Acting School. Theatre includes: *Just Like Real Life* (Latitude Festival); *Mary's Babies* (Vault Festival); *I Have A Mouth And I Will Scream* (Vault Festival/The Bunker); *The Lady And the Unicorn* (Yard Theatre); *Acorn* (Courtyard Theatre); *After Penelope* (The White Bear Theatre/RADA Festival/Rome International Festival); *It Felt Like A Kiss* (Punchdrunk/MIF). Film: *A Drop of Ambition* (short), *The Outer Circle* (winner of the Pears short film fund 2017). Audio: *Doctor Who*.

KAI SPELLMAN - ASHER/ MOSHER/DAVID
Kai trained at Masters Performing Arts College where he achieved a degree in Musical Theatre. He has since become an accomplished actor and writer.
Theatre credits include: *Slaves of Solitude* (Hampstead Theatre); *Romeo and Juliet* (Italy Tour); *Imogen* (Shakespeare's Globe); *Laurence After Arabia* (Hampstead Theatre); *West Side Story* and *The Wizard of Oz* (Spanish Tour); *To Paint the Earth* (Southwark Playhouse).
Television credits include: *Humans* (Series 2 – Channel 4).

CREATIVE LIST

MAYA ELLIS - PRODUCER

Maya is a theatre producer, administrator and programmer. Alongside producing she currently works for Summerhall in Edinburgh and Clean Break.

Producing credits include: *Whalebone* (Edinburgh Festival Fringe); *Moonfleece* (The Pleasance); *How The Vote Was Won* (The Bunker), *Byron: Angel and Outcast* (Cadogan Hall); and *Stop and Search* (Arcola).

KERRY KYRIACOS MICHAEL - DIRECTOR AND DESIGNER

Kerry, a second generation North London Cypriot, was Artistic Director & Chief Executive of Theatre Royal Stratford East from Sept 2004 to Sept 2017. For thirteen years, he forged the Theatre's commitment to developing new work and championing voices under-represented in the mainstream. In March 2018 Kerry won Artistic Director of The Year at the OFF WEST END Awards, in April he was awarded the Freedom of the City of London and awarded an MBE in the Queen's Birthday Honours List of 2018.

Kerry's recent theatre-directing highlights include: *Aladdin* at the New Wimbledon Theatre staring Paul Merton; a new production of *The Who's Tommy* – embedding creative British Sign Language, Captioning and Audio Description (Winner UK Theatre Awards Best Touring Production '17); Ray Davies' *Come Dancing* (Winner What's On Stage Best New Musical); *The Harder They Come* (transferred to the West End and tours of Canada and USA); Tanika Gupta's play *Love N Stuff* which he also designed; Cosh Omar's plays *The Battle of Green Lanes* and *The Great Extension*; John Adam's opera, *I Was Looking At The Ceiling and Then I Saw The Sky* (co-production with Barbican Centre).

YASMIN PAIGE - ASSISTANT DIRECTOR

Yasmin is an Actor and Assistant Director. She has six years of theatre experience, performing most notably at the Palace Theatre, Young Vic, and the Royal Court. She has also worked in film and television (*Submarine, Pramface*). She studied English Literature at Queen Mary University of London where she researched and studied the Palestine/Israeli conflict through the literature of prominent Israeli and Palestinian writers.

KIT HINCHCLIFFE - ASSOCIATE DESIGNER

Kit studied Performance Design and Practice at Central St Martins College of Art and Design. She is the Joint Artistic Director of Lidless Theatre for which her credit include: *The Wasteland*; *Pebbles*; *They Have Long Arms and They Can Find Me* and *Moonfleece*. She has also designed for companies including Jethro Compton, Robin Howard Dance Theatre, Exploding Whale, Anders Duckworth and Ciemulator Dance Theatre. She is also a key member of the team at the Architecture Social Club. More information on Lidless can be found here: www.lidlesstheatre.com

WILL MONKS - PROJECTION AND LIGHTING DESIGNER

Will trained at Bristol Old Vic Theatre School.
Theatre includes: *Jericho's Rose* (Hope Theatre); *Trojan Horse* (Summerhall, Edinburgh; winner of Fringe First and Amnesty International Freedom of Expression Awards); *The Dark Room* (Theatre503; nominated for Best Lighting Designer: Offie Award); *The Boy, the Piano and the Beach*; *On the Outskirts of a Large Event*; *Who Cares*; *Dust*; *Bare Skin On Briny Waters*; *E15*; *I Am Joan, Tanja* (UK tours); *We Live By The Sea* (nominated for Best Ensemble and Best Production: Offie Awards); *This Is Where We Live* (international tours); *Dyl* (Old Red Lion); *The Benidorm Elvis Fiesta* (Benidorm Palace); *Chilcot* (The Lowry, Battersea Arts Centre); *Dangerous Or Otherwise*; *How To Survive The Blitz And Other Things, Time Passes. Listen.* (site specific); *The Secret Slowness Of Movement* (David Roberts Art Foundation).

MUNOTIDA CHINYANGA – SOUND DESIGNER

Munotida Chinyanga is a sound designer and director. She trained in Theatre Arts (BA and MA) at Middlesex University along with The Almeida Theatre and the Young Vic's Director Training Programme.

Credits for sound design include: *A Small Place* (The Gate Theatre); *Wings* (Oxford Northwall).

Directing credits include: *Gilgamesh* (The National Theatre of Rome), *Five Plays* (Young Vic); *unPlaying* (The Brookmill Gallery); *Catalyst* (Oxford Northwall).

DEVIKA RAMCHARAN – STAGE MANAGER

Devika Ramcharan trained at the Royal Central School of Speech and Drama.

Theatre includes: for Theatre Royal Bath's Ustinov Studio as CSM; *Blue Door. A*s ASM; *The Whale; The Open House; The Mentor.* As SM; *Kettle of Fish (*The Yard). Additional ASM credits include; *Wake* (Birmingham Opera); *Pity* (The Royal Court); *Les Misérables* (Pimlico Opera); *Another World* (The National Theatre).

LIZ HYDER – PR

Liz is an experienced workshop leader and writer. In early 2018, she won Moniack Mhor's Emerging Writer Award for her debut novel, *Bearmouth*, which will be published by Pushkin Press in hardback in the autumn of 2019. As a freelance-multi award-winning PR Consultant working in the arts (publishing, theatre, broadcast and festivals), she's worked with household name authors, broadcasters, performers and presenters over the past fifteen years.

ACKNOWLEDGMENTS

Ali and Dahlia has been touched by many people, to whom I would like to show my gratitude:

I would like to thank my director, Kerry Kyriacos Michael for bringing this story to the stage for me. Thank you Kerry for your infectious love of story-telling and characters, your determined approach to your work, and your friendship, mentorship and guidance towards me as a new writer.

Waj Ali, Deli Segal, and Kai Spellman: You are three beautiful and talented artists who brought life into these characters and transformed them beyond my own imagination. It was a joy observing you in rehearsals as you took ownership of this story.

Thank you to Nic Connaughton at the Pleasance Theatre for taking a leap of faith with this play and pushing for it to be staged. Your support was invaluable.

Ali and Dahlia had two public readings as part of the Arcola Theatre's PlayWROUGHT Festival and HighTide Festival. Thank you to both festivals for supporting new writing. And thank you to the wonderful artists and creatives who gave their time and talents to these important initial stages.

Thank you to our producer and wonderful production team of creatives who have worked tirelessly throughout rehearsals and into production. And to the lovely Liz Hyder for our PR.

Thank you to Steven Greenhalgh and everyone at Samuel French for your constant support throughout the publishing process. Also thank you, Emma Anacootee-Parmar for guiding me during each step and dealing with my constant edits.

Thank you to Akram Khan and everyone at AKC for their love and support throughout my creative journey.

Thank you to the wonderful Iman Aoun, her creative team, and the students of Ashtar Theatre in Ramallah, who welcomed and embraced me in Palestine.

Thank you also to Nick Kent, Lucy Dunkerley of Border Crossings, Wolf Rabstein, Aml El-Houderi, and Osama Munajjed.

Thank you to my sister, for her love and support for this story throughout.

And finally, thank you to my mother.

FIRST PERFORMANCE INFO

Ali and Dahlia was first performed at The Pleasance Theatre, London from 26th March until 14th April.

This production was kindly supported by the Arts Council England.

CHARACTERS

ALI: A Palestinian from Bir Nabala.
DAHLIA: An Israeli from Jerusalem.
MOSHE / ASHER / DAVID: An officer / Dahlia's brother /
An IDF soldier.

ALI and DAHLIA age from 14 to 30 years old.
ASHER ages from 13–21 years old.
(Asher does not appear in the present.)

All ages are played by the same actors.

Scene One

Projected footage: Video footage spanning from the late 1800's to present day. Including but not limited to: Ottoman rule; British Mandate Palestine; 1948 declaration of the State of Israel; the Six-Day War; the First Intifada; the Oslo Accords; the Second Intifada; suicide bombings in Israel; the bombardment of Gaza; and finally news footage of the US embassy relocated to Jerusalem.

May 2018. Al-Jalame Prison. A dimly lit interrogation room. ALI, *thirty, is hooded, and stands centre stage. Two chairs sit upstage.* ALI *holds a stress pose: his arms outstretched wide with his knees bent and heels raised. An officer,* MOSHE, *thirty four, is also in the room.*

MOSHE Take it off.

ALI, *exhausted, takes his hood off. He looks disheveled. He retreats back, covering his eyes due to the bright light.*

Lower your hands. I want to see your face.

ALI *lowers his hands.*

What is your name?

ALI Omar Nasser.

MOSHE How old are you, Omar?

ALI Thirty.

MOSHE Do you know why you are here?

ALI Yes.

MOSHE Tell me why.

ALI I entered Jerusalem.

MOSHE And... *(Pause)* I'm waiting.

ALI I entered Jerusalem...

MOSHE *Illegally.* 'I entered Jerusalem illegally.' There! Say it.

ALI I entered Jerusalem illegally.

MOSHE Good. Why did you enter Jerusalem *illegally*?

ALI The American Embassy.

MOSHE Yes? The American Embassy, what about it?

ALI I went there to protest the / illegality of the—

MOSHE No! No! No! This is not what we fucking rehearsed! Don't give me this UN bullshit. You went there to throw rocks. Say it with me. *I threw rocks*

ALI I threw rocks.

MOSHE Bravo! I threw rocks with the *intention*—say that little word for me. *Intention*.

ALI Intention.

MOSHE I threw rocks with the *intention* of harming Israeli citizens. Say it!

   ALI *spits aggressively towards* MOSHE.

MOSHE Clean it up! I said clean up your mess!

   ALI *starts to wipe the floor with his hands.*

MOSHE When I arrive home, the first thing my daughters do is run and jump up into my arms. Sometimes, they have not seen their father for three days straight. I can't even call them to tell them when their *aba* will be home because people like you are unpredictable. And you know the first thing my girls say to me when they are in my arms? 'Aba, your shirt is wet. It's soaking, aba. Eurgh, it's disgusting, Aba.' *(Beat)* No more!

ALI I threw rocks with the intention to harm Israeli citiziens. Now, let me go!

MOSHE *(laughing)* Sure, whatever you want. You want me to order you an Uber? I have to make sure you are not a threat to Israel, Omar.

ALI I'm not a threat!

MOSHE Really? All that Arab blood like a hotbed of hate inside of you. You're angry, you're filled with rage. And you can't control this rage, so you strap a bomb to your body, get on a crowded bus in Jerusalem and... Boom. I would feel a great sense of guilt if this were to happen. *(Beat)* Now, let's continue. After entering Israel, illegally, you were arrested in the vicinity of Jerusalem's Old City, correct?

ALI Yes.

MOSHE You tried to make your way to the American Embassy, correct?

ALI Yes.

MOSHE You were seized by IDF soldiers. You resisted arrest didn't you? Say it for me.

ALI I resisted arrest.

MOSHE Good. The judge will ask you the following. Did you climb an eight-metre-high concrete wall?

ALI Yes.

MOSHE Stretching seven-hunded and eight kilometres across?

ALI Yes.

MOSHE With razor wire, checkpoints, gun towers and an electronic monitoring system?

ALI Yes.

MOSHE So you could see with your own eyes it was forbidden?

ALI Yes.

MOSHE Did you have a permit to enter Israel?

ALI No.

MOSHE Therefore, you broke the rules, correct?

ALI Yes.

MOSHE One more time, Omar. Tell the judge, you broke the rules. Did you break the rules, Omar?

ALI Yes. Yes. YES! I broke the rules. I broke the rules. I climbed over that like I was fucking Spiderman!

> **MOSHE** *shoves* **ALI** *to the floor.*

MOSHE Get up! Get up! Get up. (**ALI** *staggers up*) Now bend your knees. Bend those knees *(In Arabic)* One day you will respect me, Omar. One day. *(In English)* Let's start again, from the beginning. What is your name? I said, what is your name?

> *Beat.*

ALI Omar Nasser.

Scene Two

A few days later. The same room. DAHLIA, *thirty, smartly dressed, is waiting. The door opens and* ALI *is pushed inside. The door closes.* ALI *is hooded and wearing standard prison provided clothes.* ALI *senses someone is in the room with him.*

DAHLIA Omar Nasser, correct?

ALI *nods his head.*

Remove the hood for me, please. I'll dim the lights to help your eyes adjust.

DAHLIA *goes behind* ALI *and dims the lights.* ALI *slowly removes his hood. He sees* DAHLIA *and recognises her. He rushes towards the door.*

Hey! Hey! Stop there! I'm a lawyer. I'm here to help you.

ALI *slowly turns around to face* DAHLIA.

Ali? *(Beat)* What are you doing here?

ALI I threw rocks with the intention to harm Israeli citizens, so I've been told.

Beat.

DAHLIA Why did you lie about your name?

Beat.

ALI You did well for yourself!

DAHLIA Excuse me?

ALI A lawyer, yes? Mabrouk. *[Arabic – Congratulations].* Your family must be proud of you.

DAHLIA Thank you.

ALI Are you nervous?

DAHLIA Do I look nervous?

ALI Yes. That's why I'm asking.

> **ALI** *takes a step towards* **DAHLIA**. *Suddenly* **DAHLIA** *rushes towards the door.* **ALI** *gets there first and blocks her exit.*

Where are you going?

DAHLIA Step away from the door.

ALI Tell me where you are going.

DAHLIA Get out of my way, Ali.

ALI Promise me—promise me, you won't--

DAHLIA Step away from the fucking door! Now!

> **ALI** *holds his hands in the air and moves away from the door towards the centre of the room.*

ALI Twenty years!

That is what they told me. Twenty years is what I could be imprisoned for. Is this true?

DAHLIA Inciting violence and stone-throwing with intent to harm can carry a sentence of up to twenty years. It's rare / but—

ALI (**ALI** *starts clapping. Proclaiming)* Well done, Israel!

DAHLIA I would take this seriously. You're going to be tried in a military court next week.

ALI A *military* court?

DAHLIA Israel runs two separate legal systems here. An Israeli settler in the West Bank is tried in the civil courts and a Palestinian in a military court.

ALI You would have thought I was a member of Hamas.

DAHLIA Are you?

ALI What?

DAHLIA Are you a member of Hamas?

ALI You think I am some militant running around shooting rockets into Israel in retaliation for—

DAHLIA Hey, hey, I'd watch your language from now on. *Retaliation.* Is that what you think it is?

ALI Oh, I'm sorry. Why don't you pick a more fitting word, Dahlia.

Beat.

DAHLIA I don't think I'm the right person for your case, Ali.

ALI You change your mind quickly. Do you do this with all your clients?

DAHLIA You don't get it do you? I can't defend you in court. I can't defend someone...

ALI Someone, what? Someone who you—fucked?

DAHLIA I'm so happy you find all of this amusing.

ALI You have to agree, this is beautiful. You couldn't make this up if you tried. It's Hollywood, Dahlia! *Two former lovers forced together in Israeli detention.* You will be played by Gal Gadot, and I will be played by Chris Pine.

DAHLIA Chris Pine's not Arab.

ALI This is my movie and I want Chris Pine to play me! If Jake Gyllenhaal can play the Prince of Persia, Chris Pine can play an Arab.

DAHLIA Ali—

ALI I wish I would have had some warning of your arrival. If I knew you were coming I would have cleaned myself up.

DAHLIA I'm not here to judge you.

ALI I hope not, because you are my lawyer. Do you have a cigarette?

DAHLIA It's not allowed.

ALI You think I care what is allowed or not? I could end up in here for twenty years. Do you have a cigarette or not?

DAHLIA *goes in her bag and takes out a pack of cigarettes. She gives one to* **ALI** *and lights it for him.*

Thank you. I would ask you to join me but I don't want to get you into trouble, lawyer.

DAHLIA *lights one for herself. They smoke in silence.*

DAHLIA How have you been?

ALI Incarcerated.

DAHLIA I mean *in general.*

ALI In general?

DAHLIA I don't know—I don't know what to say, here.

ALI In general, I am wonderful as you can see. How are you, *in general?*

DAHLIA I'm fine.

ALI Good. We've both concluded that the two of us are, *in general,* fine. *(Pause)* Are you any good at this?

DAHLIA Good at what?

ALI Your job. Can you get me free?

DAHLIA I would first need to ascertain the circumstances around your arrest. What was your motivation—

ALI Donald Trump.

DAHLIA Excuse me?

ALI Donald Trump. You wanted a motivation. You have one. A sociopathic cunt!

DAHLIA What?

ALI Do you disagree with me?

DAHLIA No... No. I just wouldn't go that far.

ALI Of course you wouldn't.

DAHLIA At least a cunt has warmth and depth.

ALI Fuck, that is *good!* Can I keep that? I'll tell the guys in the cells opposite me.

DAHLIA Why did you go to Jerusalem? You knew there would be trouble that day. What did you think you would achieve by trying to get to the embassy?

ALI Revenge.

DAHLIA You can't use words like *revenge* in court.

ALI Of course, I'm sorry, I forgot. *An eye for an eye.* How's that for the judge?

DAHLIA Will you stop fucking around. You can't justify revenge to a judge.

ALI 'Your honour, my client sought revenge for the civilians slaughtered along the Gaza border, including the medical personnel shot in the neck while trying to rescue the injured, following the opening of the US embassy.' It's not just a building, Dahlia. It's what it stands for. 14th May 1948, the State of Israel was declared—

DAHLIA I wasn't aware of that. Thank you.

ALI I'm not finished. 14th May 2018, and America announces to the world that it officially recognises Jerusalem as Israel's capital! Seventy years to the day! They did it to taunt us. They know what that day means to us. /The Naqba!

DAHLIA The Naqba, yes.

Beat.

ALI Who put you up to this?

DAHLIA What are you talking about?

ALI You're not a lawyer. Don't play with me.

DAHLIA You've gone mad!

ALI Don't lie to me, Dahlia. You never talked about *law*. You never talked about all of this. They brought you in here to break me down, didn't they?

DAHLIA What? Don't be ridiculous.

ALI They know all about us. I know how they work, I'm not stupid! What have you told them about me? / How much have they paid you?

DAHLIA Told them? You're crazy. / I didn't even know I would see you today.

ALI Don't lie to me, Dahlia! / Tell me what you've said to them!

DAHLIA Enough! Enough of this! They know nothing about us and we're going to keep it that way! Do you understand? Now sit down. Sit down, I said!

ALI *takes a moment and then sits.*

Thank you.

Pause.

Have you eaten anything?

ALI Yes! They hired Yotam Ottolenghi to devise the special menu for the prisoners. It was fucking mouth-watering.

DAHLIA *goes into her bag and takes out a wrapped-up homemade sandwich which she throws to* ALI.

What's this?

DAHLIA It's my lunch.

ALI *unwraps it and inspects the sandwich by pulling it apart; meticulously scanning its contents.*

What do you think you're doing?

ALI Inspecting it.

DAHLIA Inspecting it for what?

ALI Anthrax.

DAHLIA You're actually insane!

ALI How do I know you are not a spy / sent to coerce me into making a false confession?

DAHLIA Do I look like a spy?

ALI Well, that's the point! If I know you're a spy then you're not a very good spy, are you?

DAHLIA Just eat the damn sandwich, Ali.

ALI No. I'm not hungry.

DAHLIA For God's sake, just eat the fucking sandwich!

Beat. **ALI** *starts eating.*

ALI Thank you. *(mocking)* For God's sake, just eat the fucking sandwich. *(Beat)* I seem to have a love-hate relationship with God at the moment. I figured if I play hard to get and *ghost* him for a while then maybe he will pay me some much needed attention.

Beat.

DAHLIA Ali, I could lose my job for not informing them. You do know this, don't you?

ALI And I could end up in prison for twenty years. I think we both have a fair amount at stake here.

(Pause)

DAHLIA Okay.

ALI Thank you.

DAHLIA I need you to be on my side and trust me. This won't work otherwise.

DAHLIA *goes to her bag and takes out her phone.*

I'll need to take some pictures of you for my records.

ALI Shall I smile in resistance or look pained by the occupation?

DAHLIA Just be normal.

ALI I'm a Palestinian, Dahlia. I'm not well-versed in normality.

DAHLIA Just look at the bloody camera.

    DAHLIA *takes pictures of* **ALI**.

ALI So who do you work for?

DAHLIA A legal team that defends Palestinians in Israeli detention.

ALI Are you part of Amnesty?

DAHLIA No.

ALI The UN?

DAHLIA No.

ALI The Palestinian Centre for Human Rights?

DAHLIA Ali!

    Beat.

ALI The ICHR?

DAHLIA Enough!

ALI So you're rather small in the grand scheme of things.

    Beat.

DAHLIA Stand up.

    DAHLIA *takes one last photo of Ali, standing.*

Can I fire you if we don't see eye to eye? You know, if I don't feel you are working for me.

DAHLIA I wouldn't advise you to do that.

ALI Why? Are you getting attached, already?

DAHLIA Clearly.

ALI I have a way with the women; so I have been told.

DAHLIA Let's start on the day of your arrest. On the 14th May, you were seized in Jerusalem. Correct?

ALI Yes. Correct.

DAHLIA You entered Jerusalem by climbing over the West Bank barrier. Yes?

ALI Yes.

DAHLIA Did you apply for a permit to cross?

ALI No. I broke the rules! I'm sorry.

DAHLIA *writes on his paperwork.*

DAHLIA Tell me what happened that day. *(Beat)* Talk or I can leave. It's up to you.

Beat.

ALI The West Bank was alive with protests. Thousands of us took to the streets and headed towards Qalandia checkpoint. It was like the Intifada all over again.

DAHLIA Describe the events at the checkpoint.

ALI It was chaos. The soldiers were shooting at us. Tear gas and rubber bullets were flying everywhere. When you get hit by one, you go down. We threw whatever we could. We set fire to bins, to tyres—

DAHLIA Why?

ALI You don't get it, do you? This was war. That embassy was an act of war against us. I saw news footage on my phone of the massacre happening along the Gaza border and the world did nothing. Where is the UN when you need them? Why don't they send an army to protect us from Israel?

DAHLIA How did it make you feel? *(Beat)* I have to ask these questions.

ALI Angry. Powerless. Because we were losing.

DAHLIA So what did you do?

ALI   There is a secluded spot where the wall is clear of watchtowers and snipers. About thirty of us climbed over with rope ladders and headed towards Jerusalem. I have never seen so many soldiers before. Thousands, lining the streets to protect that building. And what did we do while Gazans were being slaughtered? We threw rocks.

Beat.

DAHLIA An IDF soldier went missing that day.

ALI *begins to laugh.*

Why do you find that funny?

ALI I apologise if my sympathy does not extend as far as yours, but it's difficult to feel it when you are looking down the barrel of their guns.

Beat.

DAHLIA I think we're finished for today.

DAHLIA *packs her bag.*

ALI Hey! I thought we had to be truthful in here! *(Beat)* I was beaten, Dahlia! You want to see the marks? I was beaten by soldiers in the street like I was a rabid dog.

DAHLIA I'm sorry. I'm sorry to hear that.

ALI I don't believe you.

DAHLIA Then don't.

DAHLIA *goes to leave.*

ALI Promise me you'll come back.

DAHLIA Goodbye, Ali.

DAHLIA *leaves. The lights start to flicker. We hear the faint sounds of bombs exploding in the distance as* ALI *remembers something. Blackout.*

Scene Three

Sixteen years earlier. 2002. Video footage plays of the Second Intifada.

We are now at a secluded part of the West Bank wall still under construction. The distant sounds of mortar shells and gunfire. Fourteen-year-old ALI *scrambles on stage and runs behind some concrete.*

DAHLIA *fourteen-years-old, wearing her school uniform, runs on stage, she drags her brother,* ASHER, *thirteen-years-old, also in uniform. She is breathless and clearly lost.* ASHER *is scared.* ALI *sees her from under the rubble and watches intently.*

ASHER *(Hebrew)* Dahlia, I want to go home. It's not safe here.

DAHLIA *(Hebrew)* Stay close to me. Everything is going to be fine.

ASHER *(Hebrew)* We should have waited for aba to arrive. I told you to stay inside school when the firing started.

DAHLIA *(Hebrew)* Shut up, Asher! I am trying to find out where we are.

DAHLIA *and* ASHER *wander. A sudden flurry of gunshots are heard.* DAHLIA *grabs* ASHER *and runs behind the same concrete block as* ALI. *All three jump out from the hiding place.* ALI *pulls out a slingshot from his pocket.* DAHLIA *and* ASHER *hold their hands up encircling* ALI.

ALI *(Arabic)* Get back. Get back. / Don't come any closer.

DAHLIA *(Hebrew)* Wait. Wait. / Don't shoot—

ALI *(Arabic)* Get away before / I shoot—

ASHER *(Hebrew)* Dahlia, Dahlia, / do something.

ALI *(Arabic)* Get away from here!

DAHLIA *(Hebrew)* Run behind the wall, Asher! / Quickly. Run!

ASHER *and* DAHLIA *run behind the incomplete wall.* ALI *aims his slingshot and fires but misses.* ALI *sets up position downstage, ready to shoot on sight. He waits.* DAHLIA *slowly pokes her head from behind the wall.* ALI *shoots.* DAHLIA *ducks behind the wall again.*

(Hebrew) Hey! Hey! Stop shooting at us and we can talk you idiot.

ASHER *pokes his head out. Another shot from* ALI. ASHER *retreats.*

ASHER *(Hebrew)* Dahlia, do something! He is crazy!

DAHLIA *(Hebrew)* Shut up, Asher! Shut up!

ALI *(Arabic)* I'll shoot you if you come out from there. I mean it. / Get out of here!

ASHER *(Hebrew)* Dahlia. Speak to him in English.

DAHLIA *(Hebrew)* Shut up, Asher! *(English, slowly at first)* Hello? Hello? I don't understand what you are saying! / Do you speak—

ALI *(Arabic)* Go away! I'm warning you!

ASHER *(Hebrew)* Speak again, Dahlia. Speak again.

DAHLIA *(Hebrew)* Keep quiet, Asher! *(English)* Hello? Listen to me! Just listen. I—can't—understand—you! Do you speak—/ English?

ALI *(English)* English!

DAHLIA Yes! Yes. English.

ALI I will shoot you! I will shoot you unless you leave here.

DAHLIA Okay! Okay! Hear me out for a moment.

DAHLIA *and* ASHER *reveal themselves.*

Now, I don't think you are much good at this shooting business. So why don't we—

ASHER *tries to run.* ALI *trips him up.*

ALI Hey! Hey!

DAHLIA Asher!

ASHER *runs back to* DAHLIA's *side.*

DAHLIA (*To Asher*) Idiot!

ASHER He hit me!

Beat.

DAHLIA We're going to leave you alone now, do you understand?

ALI Go back the way you came!

DAHLIA We will be going very soon, won't we, Asher? (ASHER *nods in agreement*) We ran from school when the firing started and ended up here. Our father will be looking for us. He will arrive here any moment now. If I can give you some advice? I would be quick and run away if I were you, because if he finds you, it will be very bad news—

ALI (*Arabic*) Shut up! You're lying! (*English*) No one is here but us.

DAHLIA Suit yourself. But we did warn you, didn't we, Asher?

ASHER We did warn you. When he finds you, you'll regret all of this. The soldiers could be with him.

ALI *lowers his slingshot. He walks towards* DAHLIA.

DAHLIA We don't want you to get hurt. You should go, quickly.

ALI (*fearful*) Okay. Okay. I will go. Thank you.

ALI *walks past* DAHLIA. DAHLIA *suddenly punches him in the stomach, sending him to the ground.* DAHLIA *grabs his slingshot as* ALI *tries to run. She grabs a stone from the ground and aims the slingshot at* ALI.

DAHLIA Get up! Put your hands up! Good. Now, turn around and face me. Asher, check his pockets.

ASHER *goes up to* ALI *and frisks him, rather awkwardly.*

ASHER Nothing. He has nothing.

ALI *(noticing blood from a cut on his elbow)* I'm bleeding. You made me bleed.

DAHLIA Not so confident now, are we? There's no-one to blame but yourself.

ASHER We told you to stop. We told you / you would regret it!

DAHLIA Asher, enough!

ASHER Okay...

DAHLIA If you are going to pretend you have the guts to try and attack us, then you had better follow through with it. Come closer to me.

ASHER Dahlia, let's go now. Aba will be worried.

DAHLIA Not until this *thing* appologises for what he did.

ALI *(Arabic)* Fuck off!

ASHER Aba said they kidnap Israelis.

DAHLIA He doesn't look dangerous to me! *(To* ALI*)* You should find out if I am a friend or enemy before shooting, don't you think? It's called manners.

ALI *(protesting)* I am manners!

ASHER *(laughs)* I *am* manners! He said 'I *am* manners!'

DAHLIA It's 'I *have* manners'. *Have*. Tell me where you are from!

ALI No!

DAHLIA Tell me or I will call the soldiers and they will lock you up. Only last week, some Arabs threw rocks at our car as my father was driving. I bet that was you, wasn't it?

ASHER They smashed the back window. The rock landed on my lap. I was lucky not to be killed!

DAHLIA Was that you? Was it?

ALI *shakes his head.*

Good. I asked you, where you are from!

ALI Jaffa.

ASHER He's lying, Dahlia. He's lying to us. He's not from Jaffa.

DAHLIA *(Hebrew)* Shut up, Asher! Shut up. *(English)* You're not from Jaffa. Jaffa's in Israel.

ASHER He's an Arab, Dahlia, they want to destroy Israel, aba says. They want drown us in the sea.

DAHLIA Is that what you want? To drown us in the sea?

ALI *shakes his head.*

Are you sure about that?

ALI *nods his head.*

DAHLIA I'll just ask the soldiers to find out where you live. Bye!

ALI No, wait, don't! Don't go! *(Beat)* I'm from Bir Nabala.

DAHLIA That wasn't so hard was it?

ASHER Dahlia, I want to go find aba now. *(Hebrew)* He looks scared enough.

DAHLIA *(Hebrew)* We will soon. Not yet. *(English)* Asher, walk up to him. Walk up to him, I said.

ASHER *nervously does what he is told. The two boys face each other in silence.*

Apologise for attacking at my brother.

ALI No.

DAHLIA Alright then. Asher, do what he did to you.

ASHER *(Hebrew)* Dahlia, stop this now!

DAHLIA He needs to learn to never do that again to us.

ASHER *(Hebrew)* No. I can't do it.

DAHLIA Then spit at him. Do something, Asher. Don't let him think you are not a man!

ASHER *(Hebrew)* No! Dahlia, enough!

DAHLIA You're so weak! Punish him, Asher!

Pause. ASHER, *in a panic, pushes* ALI *and then runs off.*

ASHER *(Hebrew)* I'm going to tell aba. I'm going to tell him what you are doing here.

ASHER *runs off.*

DAHLIA Asher! Asher! Come back now! *(Hebrew)* It's not safe! Asher! *(Beat) (English)* He's so embarrassing.

ALI *laughs to himself.*

Don't laugh.

Pause.

(pointing) I live there. In Ramot. I was staying near the Park Hotel when the suicide bomber attacked it. He killed thirty people. He was dressed as a woman, you know. He did it during the Passover seder. Why would he do that? I also saw the Megiddo Junction bus bombing. I watched it on the news with my mother. You know, when I'm eighteen, I will start my military service and protect Israel from all the terrorists. My friend's brother, Ilan, is stationed near Ashkelon. He was sent to Jenin. She told me he visited home last week and said, Hamas and the PLO are losing. So I'd change sides if I were you.

ALI No.

DAHLIA No? You don't look like you could fight in any army to me.

ALI I can fight! I can fight!

DAHLIA You tried to shoot me just now but you aren't very skilled at it. You're not even good at lying. I've been to Jaffa many times you know, so you wouldn't have been able to trick me into believing otherwise.

ALI My grandparents' home is in Jaffa!

DAHLIA Where?

ALI I don't know.

DAHLIA See! All lies!

ALI It's not a lie! They left Jaffa after the Naqba. Everybody left. They left their home but one day I will return. I have the key to prove it.

DAHLIA Show me!

ALI No.

Beat.

DAHLIA How old are you?

ALI Fourteen.

DAHLIA Me too... I'm Dahlia. You might as well tell me your name now.

ALI Ali.

DAHLIA Here, this is yours. *(She hands* ALI *the slingshot)* You know, when they finish the wall, they say it will be twice the size of the Berlin Wall. My father says, the wall will help keep Israel safe.

ALI My father says, 'nearly everything in the world is made in China; except courage, this is made in Palestine!'

DAHLIA *wanders behind the gap in the wall and shouts out.*

DAHLIA This is Israel! *(She wanders back to* ALI*)* And this is...

ALI Palestine.

DAHLIA Exactly. There won't need to be any more fighting once it's finished. I will have Israel and you will have Palestine. Agreed?

ALI Palestine! (ALI *wanders to the other side of the wall and stops, shouts out*) Palestine!

DAHLIA No. You can't have it all.

ALI We were here first.

DAHLIA No, we have been here for over three thousand years. If you don't like it then leave. The Jews only have one homeland. Do you know how many the Arabs have? Twenty two. That's not exactly fair is it?

ALI *reluctantly walks from one side of the wall to the other.*

ALI Israel... Palestine...

DAHLIA See, that wasn't so difficult. (*Beat*) Do you go to school?

ALI School is closed down because it got hit last month. Books are boring anyway. Now, I help my father in the shop.

DAHLIA Books aren't boring. Everything you ever need to know in your life, you can learn from a book. Ms Goldman taught us that. (DAHLIA *takes a book out of her bag and holds it out*) Here, I've just finished this in English. It's called *Treasure Island*. Can you read English?

ALI A bit.

DAHLIA What's your favourite book?

ALI *alf laylah wa-laylah [A Thousand and One Nights].*

DAHLIA What?

ALI Al'adin!

DAHLIA Well take it! It's an action adventure. Keep it for as long as you want. I won't charge a late penalty like they do in the library. Take it!

ALI *(reluctantly taking it)* Thank you.

Beat.

DAHLIA Ask me a question.

ALI What?

DAHLIA For example, what's your favourite food?

ALI Kanafeh! When we throw stones at the tanks, the soldiers chase us and we run into Hassan's bakery and he hides us in the kitchen. He has a big fridge that we hide behind. They never catch us. When the soldiers go, he gives us all the Kanafeh we can eat.

DAHLIA It's my turn!

ALI What's your favourite food?

DAHLIA You can't use the example question I asked you.

ALI Why not?

DAHLIA Because those are the rules. You have to follow the rules.

ALI Anything, yes? *(Beat)* Do you have a boyfriend?

DAHLIA That's none of your business.

ALI You said I could ask anything—

DAHLIA Next question!

ALI What do you want to become after school?

DAHLIA I want to be a writer. Ms Goldman teaches us all about literature and history. I can read Shakespeare, you know!

ALI Sheikh Sabir? He is a Sheikh?

DAHLIA No, stupid. William Shakespeare. He's a playwright. I learnt all about him. He wrote thirty-seven plays, and he didn't even have electricity.

ALI Did the soldiers cut it off?

DAHLIA What? No! It wasn't even invented back then, stupid. Tell me what *you* want to be when you grow up. Tell me.

ALI No. You will laugh.

DAHLIA I won't—I promise. How can I trust you when you are not honest with me? What do you want to be?

Beat.

ALI *(quietly)* Gene Kelly!

DAHLIA What?

ALI Gene Kelly... Gene Kelly!

DAHLIA Yes, yes I heard you—

ALI Gene Kelly is the most gifted man in the world. *An American in Paris. On the Town. Singin' in the Rain. (Beat)* No? Oh! When you watch Gene Kelly, you forget where you are. Everything just stops. Time just stops. When the tanks drive past my home, I watch Gene Kelly and he is free! He could run up this wall and jump over it if he wanted to.

DAHLIA Don't be ridiculous.

ALI I'll show you one day! Gene Kelly is the best. *(Beat)* And Mr Bean. He's funny you know.

DAHLIA Mr Bean?

ALI does a mock Mr Bean impression. DAHLIA is confused.

ALI Do you live under the ground or something? You have Charlie Chaplin—

DAHLIA Oh, I know him—

ALI Then you have Mr Bean!

Beat.

DAHLIA I can show you my favourite ice-cream shop, if you like. Gideon's Gelato. They have bubblegum flavour ice-cream.

I'd have to teach you Hebrew, because Mr Gideon's English is terrible.

ALI I speak Hebrew. I don't need you to teach me. *(*ALI *shouts out Hebrew profanities with gusto)* Tistom-tah-peh! *[Shut the fuck up]* Ben zonah! *[Son of a bitch]*

DAHLIA Where did you learn that?

ALI You hear the soldiers all the time. I shout it to them! Chati charrah! *[Piece of shit]*

DAHLIA *(correcting him)* ChatiCHAT charrah

ALI Chatichat charrah! Good, yes?

Beat.

DAHLIA Maniak! *[Bastard]*

ALI Maniak!

The swearing continues for a while and the two indulge in Hebrew profanities before exploding into laughter. The laughter is broken by the sounds of distant gunfire.

DAHLIA I should go!

ALI Thank you for the book. When you come again, I will give you a Gene Kelly VHS. Deal?

DAHLIA Deal.

They shake hands. Distant gunfire continues as DAHLIA *exits.* ALI *wanders between the incompete wall.*

ALI Palestine... Palestine.

The gunfire continues. ALI *exits.*

Scene Four

*A few months later. The gap in the wall has gotten
smaller.* ALI *is standing centre stage, while* DAHLIA
is sat watching him. ALI *breaks out into monologue,
performing melodramatically, gesticulating rather
grandly, and mispronouncing most of it.*

ALI   But, soft! What light through yonder window breaks?

It is the east, and Juliet is the sun.

Arise, fair sun, and kill the envious moon,

Who is already sick and pale with grief,

That thou her maid art far more fair than she:

Be not her maid, since she is envious;

Pause.

DAHLIA *(prompting)* Her vestal livery is but sick and green

ALI *shushes* DAHLIA.

ALI   Her vestal livery is but sick and green

And none but fools do wear it; cast it off.

It is my lady, O, it is my love!

O, that she knew she were!

Beat.

How was that?

DAHLIA *(clapping)* Bravo, bravo!

ALI   How were my emotions?

DAHLIA I believed every word.

ALI   What about my articulation? I read that this is very
important in Shakespeare.

DAHLIA If you keep practising, I can see you playing Romeo
on the stage one day.

ALI Really? You think so?

DAHLIA Absolutely. You will perform on a stage in Tel Aviv, maybe for the Habima, and I will have a front row seat!

ALI No, I want to make movies!

Pause.

I have got a surprise for you.

DAHLIA What is it?

ALI You'll see soon... (**ALI** *checks his watch*)

DAHLIA I don't know how you do it. One whole month of fasting! Yom Kippur only requires one day.

ALI *takes some water and a date from his bag and breaks his fast.*

ALI *(Arabic) O Lord, I have fast for you, I believe in you, I trust and depend on you, and I break my fast with the food you have provided.*

DAHLIA I skipped Yom Kippur once by eating in my room. My mother caught me and made out the world was going to end. (*takes some food from her bag*) Here, I brought some gefilte fish and knish that my mum made for dinner last night. She doesn't suspect anything, so don't worry.

ALI *(Taking food out of his bag)* I went into the kitchen at my father's shop and took some kebabs, olives, fatayer, musakhan, and hummus. I have to be careful. (**ALI** *presents a little box*) And this is just for you. Kanafeh from Hassan's Bakery—the best bakery in the West Bank.

DAHLIA Why's it the best?

ALI It's been hit by three rockets, two tanks and one airstrike and it's still standing.

DAHLIA Really?

ALI Sa'ten! *[Arabic equivalent of bon appetit.]*

DAHLIA Sa'ten!

They start to eat together.

ALI Dahlia, I told my father I want to go to America and become a famous actor and he laughed at me. He said that acting is not a proper job. Actors don't make any money. I told him that Gene Kelly made millions. But he said, I am not and will never be Gene Kelly. Then he went to his room all angry and started talking to my mother for two hours.

DAHLIA To your mother?

ALI To her picture on the wall. One day we will return to Jaffa and I will take her back with us and rebury her in our garden.

Beat.

DAHLIA Have you ever seen your house in Jaffa?

ALI Yes.

DAHLIA But you've never been there.

ALI *produces some pictures from his bag. He shows them to* DAHLIA.

ALI Look, I have these! (*Beat*) Our garden has an orange grove. My grandfather used to send oranges all over the Middle East and beyond. Jaffa was famous! I even have postcards to prove it. They say, 'Fly KLM to Palestine!' At the back of our garden there is a one-thousand-year-old olive tree. It grows the biggest, juiciest, tastiest olives in the world. I will start up the family business. And also be an actor! (*Beat*) If you look hard, in the distance, you can see the sea. Look.

Beat.

DAHLIA Have you ever seen the sea?

ALI No.

DAHLIA Well... One day we will go together! You can come to our house by the beach—

ALI You have two houses?

DAHLIA My grandparents left it to us. Our garden looks out
into the sea. We sometimes drive down for the weekend
and spend Shabbat there.

ALI Shabbat?

DAHLIA It's great because all we do is rest, pray, play, and eat.
Work is forbidden. I reckon HaShem was bored one day
and was too lazy to go to work and said, 'Hey, people, take a
day of rest,' and then that way he could get more followers.
That's a good business incentive, right there.

ALI But what about your family?

DAHLIA It doesn't always have to be a secret—just until it's
safe. Hey, you can break challah with us.

ALI Break a what?

DAHLIA Challah. It's bread that we eat to commemorate manna
falling from the heavens for the Israelites. My favourite
part is when the drinks are poured. Our local rabbi joins us
sometimes and he usually drinks way too much wine, and
me and my friends laugh as he slurs his words over prayer.
Then every now and again we lift up our drinks—and we
shout, L'chaim!

ALI *picks up his drink.*

ALI L'chaim! Like this?

DAHLIA Yeah, that's it.

ALI L'CHAIM! It's good, right?

DAHLIA Yes.

BOTH L'CHAIM! L'CHAIM!

They drink together. Beat.

ALI Am I a Jew now?

DAHLIA Of course not. If it was that easy, everyone would become one.

Beat.

ALI Yes, that's it, Dahlia! That's what I will do. I will become a Jew!

DAHLIA What are you talking about?

ALI It might work. What would I have to do to become a Jew?

DAHLIA But you're Muslim.

ALI I know. I know this. But what if I wanted to be both? A Jew and a Muslim.

DAHLIA It doesn't work like that. It's just greedy.

ALI No, no, hear me out. I will become a Jew for *transportation purposes* only. That's it! Then I can come to your home! The soldiers will not give me any problems. I can see my house in Jaffa... I can meet your family, we can visit your house by the beach, and I will finally see the sea!

DAHLIA And if the soldiers catch you out. What will you say then?

ALI I will say... Erm... I will say...

DAHLIA See, it's a flawed plan.

ALI No. I will say... I will say, Abraham had two sons—Isaac and Ishmael! Isaac gave birth to the Jews and Ishmael gave birth to the Muslims. It's quite simple! So I can pray in a Synagogue, or a Mosque. They both lead to the same God! Any good?

DAHLIA Actually, Abraham had Isaac with his wife Sarah but he had Ishmael with his maid. So Ishmael was illegitimate. Ms Goldman told us that. Anyway, if you did want to become a Jew, you would need to have your bar mitzvah.

ALI Easy. I can do it. No problemo! I will do it now! I will become a Jew. Dahlia! Make me a Jew!

DAHLIA What? I can't do it! I'm sure it's forbidden anyway.

ALI Just give me a bar mitzvah. Come on!

DAHLIA I don't know how! I remember, you say a blessing over the Torah; it's called the aliyah. But I don't know—

ALI Say it. Say it for me.

DAHLIA I can't. I don't know all the words—

ALI It doesn't matter! I don't need to be a full Jew, you know. Just Jew-ish. Come on! Please. Say it! Just say it.

DAHLIA Fine. Fine. If it shuts you up. I don't think this is going to work and if I get punished for—

ALI SAAAAAY IT!!!!!!!!

DAHLIA Just shut up! Repeat after me! *(Hebrew)* Bless the Lord who is blessed. Blessed be the Lord who is blessed for all eternity. Blessed are You, Lord our God, King of the universe, who has chosen us from among all the nations and given us his Torah. Blessed are You, Lord, who gives the Torah. Amen.

DAHLIA recites the blessing in Hebrew which ALI repeats a few words at a time, making multiple mistakes.

Then the Torah is read aloud.

ALI Let's skip that bit.

DAHLIA Then the father finishes by saying the following: *(ALI closes his eyes momentarily) (Hebrew)* Blessed be he who has released me from being punishable for this boy.

Silence. ALI opens his eyes and looks down at his hands and body, majestically.

I told you it was a stupid idea.

ALI No. Wait a minute. Wait... *(ALI touches his body. Beat.)* I feel Jewish!

DAHLIA Don't play games, Ali. It's a not a joke.

ALI No. No. I feel Jewish.

DAHLIA Seriously?

ALI Yes, yes, I feel—different. *Jewish*. Dahlia, I think it worked! I think I'm Jewish.

DAHLIA Let's give you a Jewish name. Jacob? (ALI *pulls a face and shakes his head. He repeats this between each name)* Adam? Eli?

ALI No, no. They won't believe me. It needs to be more... More Jewish.

DAHLIA More Jewish? Menachem? Zacchaeus? Yitzhak? Gideon—

ALI Wait, wait—stop! Yitzhak! My name will be Yitzhak!

DAHLIA *(giggling)* Welcome, Yitzhak.

ALI *walks around the space with his head held high in a regal fashion.*

ALI I am Yitzhak and you, Israeli soldier, will let me pass! Out of my way now before I smash down your wall! *(Beat)* Okay, now tell me what it's like in Jerusalem to prepare me for my return.

DAHLIA It's like stepping back in time. When you travel through the Old City you pass buildings that are ancient. *(Beat)* In Jaffa, the sand reminds you of tiny grains of gold and in the distance if you look hard enough you can see the peaks of the buildings in Tel Aviv—they look like soldiers on parade. Tall and enormous. So tall they look like they pierce the clouds—

ALI Stop! Start at the beginning. Show it to me. Tell me how I will travel. What bus I will arrive on?

DAHLIA You will arrive on the number twenty five bus which heads towards Jaffa.

ALI What colour is the bus?

DAHLIA White.

ALI Is it just white, or is it off-white? White with a red border even! I need details, here!

DAHLIA White, with a green trim. This bus has a poster on it, advertising Coca-Cola. You sit in the middle of the bus and you are surrounded by people heading to Jaffa for the weekend. You are wearing a suit. You look very smart.

ALI What type of suit am I wearing?

DAHLIA It's navy blue. Slim fitted. And you wear shiny black shoes. The passengers on the bus think you look like a famous film star.

ALI Which one?

DAHLIA Gene Kelly.

ALI Yes! Yes! Gene Kelly. I knew it!

DAHLIA You take off your jacket and fold it over your arm. Well, do it!

ALI No, that's alright. I want to keep it on for you to see it when I arrive. Gene Kelly would keep his jacket on, so I'm keeping my jacket on.

DAHLIA Fine then! Keep it on. *(Beat)* On the bus you pass Tel Aviv University. Next you pass Rabin Square, named after Israel's fifth Prime Minister. After this you pass—

ALI Wait, wait... (ALI *focuses his eyes out front)* Okay, I see it, continue—

DAHLIA After this you pass King George street, then Carmel Market and finally you arrive in Jaffa. You step off the bus. You won't see the sea yet but you can smell the salt water carried with the sea breeze.

ALI *takes a deep breath and looks around taking everything in.*

ALI I can smell it, Dahlia. The sea. I'm home... Where are you? I don't see you.

DAHLIA I'm by the bus terminal. I'm wearing red shorts and a white T-shirt. I'm waving at you, can't you see me?

ALI Wait... Oh yes. I can see you now. I wave back.

DAHLIA You run towards me and then—

ALI We hug!

DAHLIA No.

ALI No?

DAHLIA You kiss me.

ALI What?

DAHLIA Are you scared?

ALI No.

DAHLIA In the story that's what happens. We can end it if you like.

ALI No. Don't end it.

ALI *kisses* DAHLIA *on the lips. Silence.*

DAHLIA We walk down to the beach. Can you see the sand in the distance? It's just across the road and behind those palm trees. Can you see it?

ALI I'm looking... I'm looking... I can't see anything, yet. Why can't I see it? I don't understand.

DAHLIA Try harder, Ali. Close your eyes and I'll count to three. Open them and you'll see it. Just try!

ALI *closes his eyes, tightly.*

One...two...three...

ALI *opens his eyes and looks out in amazement. He is clearly seeing something that only he can see. He starts to tear up. To him this is real. He looks to* **DAHLIA** *and smiles.* **ALI** *continues to look out, mesmerised while the lullaby Shlof Mayn Feygele plays.*

Scene Five

Interrogation room. 2018. Three days after Scene Two.
ALI *is eating some food out of a tupperware container.*
Something **DAHLIA** *has brought for him.* **DAHLIA** *holds*
up some head-shots, one at a time.

DAHLIA Ahmed Darwaza.

ALI No.

DAHLIA Omar Faruqi.

ALI No.

DAHLIA Yousef Hadawi. Yousef Hadawi—

ALI Are we still friends?

DAHLIA What?

ALI On Facebook. Are we still friends on Facebook?

DAHLIA Why are you asking me this?

ALI Last time I checked, we weren't friends. We had been de-friended.

DAHLIA I don't know what you are talking about.

ALI Who de-friended who?

DAHLIA Yousef Hadawi.

ALI Wait a minute—I think it was you. You de-friended me. That was it.

DAHLIA Is this for real? You're going to be standing in front of a judge next week and you're more concerned with who de-friended who on Facebook. Yousef Hadawi—yes or no?

ALI I'm just curious. What was the reason you de-friended me?

DAHLIA I didn't fucking de-friend you. I deleted my account.

ALI Because of me?

DAHLIA Don't flatter yourself. Yousef Hadawi.

ALI *(looking at the photo)* No.

DAHLIA Ishmail Darwish.

ALI Can I ask you a personal question?

DAHLIA No—

ALI Are you *single, married,* or is it *complicated?*

DAHLIA Ishmail Darwish.

ALI I thought we have to be open in here. No secrets allowed.

DAHLIA Whether I'm in a relationship or not has nothing to do with your case. Ishmail Darwish.

ALI No.

DAHLIA Yahya Mohammad. Ali, look at the photo. Yahya Mohammad.

    ALI *stares at the photo.*

ALI No. *(Beat)* Wait a minute—wait...

    ALI *takes the picture off* **DAHLIA**.

DAHLIA What? Do you know him?

ALI Yes. I know him, Dahlia.

DAHLIA Where do you know him from?

ALI Oh my God. I don't believe it!

DAHLIA What is it?

ALI It's—it's him... It's Omar Sharif!

DAHLIA Will you take this seriously?

ALI I am taking this extremely seriously! Look at his moustache. Look at those high cheekbones. This man is definitely Omar Sharif. Wait a minute... Are you telling me Omar Sharif is a member of Hamas?

DAHLIA You're full of shit, you know that!

ALI Is watching 'Lawrence of Arabia' incriminating? I've seen it multiple times.

DAHLIA *starts to pack her paperwork away.*

DAHLIA You're wasting my time. A soldier is missing; these men were seen in the vicinity—

ALI I don't care about a soldier.

DAHLIA This is an eighteen year old kid who hasn't even been to university.

ALI No. They stopped being kids the moment they picked up a gun.

DAHLIA They don't have a choice. They can't be held accountable for a political system that they are born and conditioned into. They have a choice between conscription and prison. He was doing his job.

ALI Like you did?

Beat.

DAHLIA What's that supposed to mean?

ALI Nothing.

DAHLIA I said, what's that supposed to mean?

Beat.

ALI Do you think the checkpoints will vanish one day? Will the West Bank wall be knocked down like they did in Berlin?

DAHLIA I believe that could happen one day, yes!

ALI And you and me could pick up a sledgehammer and break through the concrete, yes? We could bring it crashing down to the ground and live as one?

DAHLIA I don't see why not!

ALI I've got an idea. You know what we need? A Palestinian Trump. I'm being serious. Someone to say fuck you to the rest of the world. You don't like the way we operate, then fuck your UN resolutions, fuck your peace plan, and fuck your Geneva Convention. Because none of that is worth shit here.

Silence.

ALI Why did you join?

DAHLIA What?

ALI You shouldn't have gone. You should have said no.

DAHLIA I had to go.

ALI You could have run away. You could have left the country.

DAHLIA Don't be ridiculous.

ALI I would have come with you.

DAHLIA You don't know what it's like for us. If you don't serve, your family are humiliated. They are abandoned by their community. *(Beat)* I tried to help you and you threw it away.

Pause.

ALI What would happen if they found out about us?

DAHLIA Are you serious?

ALI Maybe it could help. *(Beat)* Tell them...

DAHLIA You want me to tell them?

ALI Tell them. Just do it.

DAHLIA No. That isn't going to happen. They can't know anything—

ALI Tell them, that we fucked against the West Bank wall during those hot summer nights.

DAHLIA You wouldn't dare.

ALI Cumming while snipers gazed through their scopes at us.

DAHLIA You're a fucking animal.

ALI There we go! Let it out, Dahlia!

DAHLIA If you try to blackmail me, I will destroy you.

ALI *(laughing)* Destroy me? Oh, I can picture the headlines now: 'Defence lawyer's Palestinian client turns out to be her illicit lover.' Tell me, Dahlia, is an Arab's circumcision any different from a Jew's?

DAHLIA *slaps* ALI *across the face.*

Aw! Fuck! You just hit me!

DAHLIA You fucking deserved it.

ALI You just—*fuck*—you hit me! You're supposed to be my lawyer and you fucking hit me. I'm your fucking client!

DAHLIA Don't you ever try to threaten me, do you understand? I don't even recognise you anymore.

ALI Then look harder.

DAHLIA What do you want from me?

ALI I want you to stay. I don't want you to leave me here.

DAHLIA *sits down.*

I'm sorry, I went too far.

Pause.

Before you saw me in here, when was the last time you thought of me?

DAHLIA Have you forgotten what you just said to me?

ALI Can I tell you when I thought of you?

DAHLIA No.

ALI That day when I climbed over; all I wanted, more than anything, was to bump into you. Even after all these years... I'm clutching stones, avoiding soldiers everywhere, and all I want is to see *you*. *(Beat)* Do you still think of me?

DAHLIA No.

ALI I don't believe you. Do you still think of me?

DAHLIA Don't do this. I warned you.

ALI I'm tired, Dahlia. I'm tired and I'm scared. I'm scared every time you leave this room because I'm afraid you won't return. *(Beat)* I'm sorry, Dahlia.

DAHLIA I'm exhausted. I want to finish for today. I just want to go home. *(Beat)* I don't want to get into this. This is all in the past.

ALI I'm sorry, Dahlia.

DAHLIA I heard you—

ALI I'm sorry, Dahlia.

DAHLIA Enough. Please. Enough.

> **DAHLIA** *walks towards the door. She stops and looks back at* **ALI***. Blackout.*

Scene Six

2007. **ASHER,** *eighteen-years-old stands in a corner of the stage. He has a bag on his shoulder. The sound of a voicemail beep.*

ASHER (*Hebrew*) Shalom. (*English*) It's Asher. Your son, in case you have forgotten. (*Beat*) I've arrived at Bakum to be processed. Ok, what to say... (*Beat*) Ima, thank you for the holishkes you made for me. I have a feeling that will be my last decent meal for a while... The bus journey was terrible. Boys my age yelling the whole time like wild animals, gloating over their achievements in sports, their accolades in High School, and their sexual accomplishments, or lack of them. And I've got thirty-two months with them. Lucky me. When I arrived the commanders herded us into the base. One boy next to me was wearing sunglasses, which they said do not bring and he ignored, so what do you think happened? They were snatched off of him and crushed beneath the commander's boots. 'How can you fight a war wearing Gucci?' What a piece of shit, eh? (*Hebrew*) Sorry ima. (*English*) You know, I wish you raised us orthodox so I could have gotten out of this on religious grounds. I was photographed for my Teudat Choger *[Military ID card]*. So no escaping now. My arms still hurt from my immunity shots. And you never told me that one would also be in my arse. I'm told not to scratch it, no matter how irritating it is. It is very irritating. I am given a lot of free stuff though to make up for all of this. Are you ready for it? A kit bag containing two medium towels, three pairs of underwear, three white vests, three pairs of army pants, three shirts, one belt, one beret, five pairs of grey socks, two pair of boots, one sweater and one winter jacket. How thoughtful. I know you warned me about opening my mouth too soon. I got into a philosophical debate with my commander over the act of war. I thought I would educate him with some Rabbi Hillel: *'What is hateful to you, do not do to your fellow. That is the whole Torah; the rest is the explanation.'* I don't think he likes me much. *(Beat)* Listen, I've got to go. Oh, by the way... I also had my fingerprints taken and my teeth were x-rayed... In case... And so tironut begins.

Scene Seven

A secluded part of the West Bank wall. 2008. The wall is now complete. DAHLIA, *twenty, is waiting. She wears military garbs and has her bags by her side.* ALI, *also twenty enters. Both stand a distance from each other and stare.*

DAHLIA Say something...

ALI I wasn't expecting to see you like this.

DAHLIA Shall I come back another time?

ALI No. No, don't go.

Beat.

DAHLIA I came straight from being discharged.

ALI Yes, I can see that!

DAHLIA Well... Aren't you going to come closer? I won't bite you. *(Beat)* Please say something, you're scaring me.

ALI I find it...

DAHLIA What?

Beat.

ALI It's actually quite sexy!

DAHLIA What?

ALI Sorry. I shouldn't have said that!

Beat.

DAHLIA Does it turn you on?

ALI A bit.

DAHLIA I won't be wearing it anymore, unless you want me to keep it for us. *(Beat)* You're late. I've been waiting here for half an hour.

ALI I was nervous. I wandered around for a while. I thought you'd go home first to see your family.

DAHLIA I told you I wanted to see you first. I told you when we spoke on the phone last week. You need to listen more.

ALI Do they know you are here?

DAHLIA No.

Beat.

ALI I missed you.

DAHLIA I don't believe you.

ALI I missed you.

DAHLIA What exactly did you miss?

ALI You want me to tell you?

DAHLIA Yes. What did you miss about me?

ALI I... I missed many things...

DAHLIA Like what? I want to know what you missed exactly.

ALI I'm worried if someone sees us like this. Can we go somewhere else?

DAHLIA I want to know what you missed about me, Ali.

ALI I missed the sound of your voice in real life and not over a phone.

DAHLIA Anything else?

ALI I missed holding you.

DAHLIA Holding me?

ALI Yes. Holding you, do you have a problem with that?

DAHLIA I mean, you're keeping quite a distance, if you missed holding me. Anything else?

ALI I missed the way you'd kiss my neck and rub my ear between your fingers.

DAHLIA What else?

ALI You're pushing it now.

DAHLIA I'm checking you haven't forgotten.

Beat.

ALI I missed the hot summer nights when you would unbutton your jeans, and you'd take my fingers to your lips; sucking on them...

DAHLIA Continue.

ALI Before... Guiding them to—

DAHLIA Guiding them? Seems a bit polite, no?

ALI Thrusting them. Is that better?

Beat.

DAHLIA Why have you not kissed me?

ALI Because you could get me killed, dressed like that. You could have me strung up by my neck. And I don't mean by Israelis. You're dangerous.

DAHLIA I thought you liked danger! I thought you liked being here with me sucking on your fingers and *thrusting* them, inside me. Have you forgotten what that feels like?

ALI No.

Beat.

DAHLIA Why did you hang up on me the other day?

ALI My father came into my room. He heard me saying 'I love you'.

DAHLIA And?

ALI 'Who is this girl who has stopped you eating my food and made you laze about all day instead of helping me serve the customers? I am ashamed to call you my son.'

DAHLIA He said that?

ALI Yes.

DAHLIA What did you say?

ALI I shout out 'Baba, I am in love with an Israeli soldier!' At first I thought he was going to kill me. I was tempted to quote a sura from the Quran! He just went silent.

'Yes, baba! Yes! I love her!' I kept smiling like a demented fool. I may have slightly pissed my pants.

DAHLIA Were you nervous?

ALI No, of course not. I was petrified.

DAHLIA And?

ALI He asked me, 'Do you even know what love is?' I told him, I can't imagine being in love with anyone else ever again.

Pause.

Did you get my present?

DAHLIA *lifts her sleeve to reveal a bracelet.*

DAHLIA This was the stupidest thing I think you have ever done. But it's beautiful. Thank you.

ALI We have the best postal service here. *FedEx Faisal*, we call him because he never fails to deliver. We have an opening where there is a hole in the concrete. We call it, *The Letterbox.* It's quite small but it's big enough for most items. Faisal lives in East Jerusalem. He waits on the other side, collects the items, and then delivers each one by hand. It's safer that way. Although now he won't do business with me anymore because you attacked him.

DAHLIA I thought he was trying to reach for my gun. I elbowed him in the face—

ALI You broke his nose.

DAHLIA No, I didn't.

ALI He screamed at me over the phone, 'This girl of yours, she almost bloody shot me, you fucker'. All I told him was to try and put the package inside your pocket without you knowing. *(Beat)* Inventive, huh?

DAHLIA You told him to put it in the pocket of an on-duty soldier at a checkpoint! I could have killed him.

ALI I thought it would be romantic. He said, 'Being in love at your age is difficult enough, but to be in love with an Israeli soldier is like digging your own grave.'

DAHLIA And what do you think?

ALI I think he's jealous! *(Beat)* Has it changed much?

DAHLIA I hardly recognised it. We used to spend so much time here.

ALI We are flooded with tourists who come and go. They love it here; taking their selfies by the wall to show their friends back home that they touched the famous West Bank wall. I've been working with my friend, Ahmed, doing West Bank tours. Hebron, Bethlehem, Ramallah, Nazareth, Sabastia; we take them all over. *(Announcing as a tour guide)* 'On our tour today you will cruise along the West Bank barrier, the most infamous wall in the world. Here, you will experience the tantalising flavours of occupation.' That's good right? I made that line up.

DAHLIA It's awful.

ALI *(performing as if for a crowd)* 'Ladies and Gentlemen, did you know that in 1799, Napoleon himself tried to seize Akka in the north from the Ottomans. It was an arduous endeavour and Napoleon fought with all his might. But when Napoleon's troops finally breached Akka's protecting wall they found the tenacious Arabs had built another wall behind it. It was then that Napoleon, fatigued and enraged, took off his hat and shot it out of a cannon into Akka, proclaiming: *(French Accent)* 'If I have failed to conquer Akka, then at least my hat will make history.' It's a true story. Then they cross over, and spend the last week of their holiday partying in Tel Aviv. *(Beat)* You know, I can recite the history of this entire land—from the Galilee to Gaza—yet I have only set foot on a quarter of it.

DAHLIA *takes out an envelope from her pocket and hands it to* **ALI**.

DAHLIA Here.

ALI What is it?

DAHLIA Just open it and you'll see.

ALI *opens the envelope and holds up a permit to enter Israel.*

It's only for a week. It was all I could get my hands on.

ALI Dahlia, it's a permit. *(Inspecting the permit)* Is it real?

DAHLIA Of course it's real. I don't have a side job making counterfeit permits.

ALI It's got my name on it. How did you get this?

DAHLIA It's yours.

ALI How did you get it?

DAHLIA I have a friend who now works for the Civil Administration's office—

ALI What? Are you crazy. You'll get arrested.

DAHLIA It's legitimate. I gave her your details and she processed it for me as a favour. *(Beat)* I want you to meet my family. I want you to visit our house by the sea, and stay with us. I want you to meet my friends. Don't you want that?

ALI Of course, I do. *(Beat)* I'm scared to fold it in case it creases... Thank you.

DAHLIA I don't want you to thank me. It's just a piece of paper.

ALI To think that a piece of paper holds so much value.

DAHLIA I'll be waiting for you at Damascus Gate.

ALI You promise?

DAHLIA Yes. I promise. *(Beat)* Ali... You still haven't kissed me yet.

> ALI *walks up to* DAHLIA. *They kiss.* ALI *picks her up and spins her around.*

Scene Eight

*2008. Four months after starting Tironut. The Hatikvah
(Israeli National Anthem) plays out loud. Asher recites
along with it. He wears the general olive-drab uniform
and beret. He picks up a drink and holds it high.*

ASHER   This is to you. This is for you my brothers. This is for
completing tironut. This is for finishing our Masa Kumta,
the beret march where no man was left behind! This is
for you Liron, and for having to carry your fucking arse
for forty-five miles. You heavy fucker! This is for all our
families who attended our Tekes Hashba'ah celebrations
with us. L'chaim. (*He drinks*) I want to ask you a question
now. Why was our Tekes Hashba'ah held in the old British
Prison in Akko? The same location where members of the
Haganah and Lehi were locked up by the British and accused
of terrorism. Why would they celebrate our achievements
there? (*Beat*) It was held in a disused prison because our
grandparents, who had arrived to the new State of Israel,
had left behind their loved ones because they believed in
one thing — a homeland for the Jews. They were locked up
and beaten by the British but they fought and they never
gave up. They fought for us all. I realise now, why we must
never give up this fight, because history tells us how that
home can be taken from you at any moment. Long live
Eretz Yisrael. Long live Eretz Yisrael.

Scene Nine

*Qalandia checkpoint: between Ramallah and Jerusalem.
The sounds of turnstiles and the clanking of metal.* ALI
stands in line looking out front. DAVID, *a young IDF
soldier in full military gear enters. He is listening to
music through his earphones.*

DAVID *(Arabic)* Move forward. Move forward. Hold up your
ID cards and permits.

> DAVID *turns to see* ALI *and takes out his earphones.*

> *(to* ALI*)* *(Arabic)* You! Wait here! Hawiya! Hawiya!
> *[Hawiya—ID card]*

> ALI *takes out his permit and ID card. He hands them to*
> DAVID. *He holds out a metal bowl and pushes it towards*
> ALI.

> Empty your pockets. *(Arabic)* Quickly, quickly!

> ALI *empties the contents of his pockets into the bowl.*

> Your name?

ALI Ali Khalidi.

DAVID Date of birth?

ALI 15th July, 1988

DAVID Father's name?

ALI Omar Khalidi.

DAVID Your mother? *(*ALI *is silent)* Hey! Are you listening?
I asked for your mother's name.

ALI Laila Farsoun.

DAVID You look nervous. Are you hiding anything?

ALI No. I'm not hiding anything.

DAVID Where do you live?

ALI Bir Nabala.

DAVID What are you planning to do in Jerusalem?

ALI I'm visiting a friend.

DAVID Who? *(No answer from* **ALI***)* What is their name?

ALI Dahlia Shavit.

DAVID What? Speak up.

ALI Dahlia Shavit.

DAVID How do you know her?

ALI She's just a friend.

DAVID You have many Jewish friends in Israel? (**ALI** *is silent*) Hey, I said, do have many Jewish friends is Israel?

ALI No. *(Beat)* Have you finished with me?

DAVID What did you say?

ALI Nothing.

DAVID I'm making conversation with you. What is your problem? Why don't you want to talk?

ALI I have given you my papers.

DAVID Why are you in a rush to leave?

ALI I want to pass, please.

> **DAVID** *starts to look over* **ALI***'s permit and ID card.* **ALI** *watches and then after a few moments puts his hands in his pockets.* **DAVID** *instinctively raises his gun.*

DAVID Hey, hey! What are you doing? Take them out. Take them out. Don't try anything with me.

ALI I'm not.

DAVID Take them out of your pocket.

ALI Why?

DAVID I said take your hands out of your pockets.

> **ALI** *slowly takes his hands out.* **DAVID** *pats* **ALI** *down.*

There's going to be no trouble today, you understand me?

ALI Yes.

> **DAVID** *holds up* **ALI**'s *ID.*

DAVID You see this? What colour ID do you have?

ALI Green.

DAVID And what is green?

ALI It's for Palestinians living in the West Bank and Gaza.

DAVID This is correct, well done. Relax, I'm not going to hurt you. What is blue for?

ALI For Palestinians living in East Jerusalem.

DAVID Correct. Why do you think this is?

ALI I don't know.

DAVID So everyone is safe! You understand? We want to keep everyone safe, don't we?

ALI Yes.

DAVID Tell me about your friend.

ALI What about her?

DAVID Is she pretty? *(Beat)* Come on, buddy. Is she pretty?

ALI Yes.

DAVID Ha ha! I bet she is! What's your type? Come on, my friend, I know you like Israeli girls. You know, I fucked an Arab-Israeli once. She was wild in bed.

ALI *(Arabic)* Fuck you!

> **DAVID** *points his gun at* **ALI**'s *head.*

DAVID Say it again! Say it again! *(Arabic)* Don't play with me. I'm trying to be friendly here. Take off your trousers. *(English)* I said take off your trousers!

ALI *takes off his shoes. He starts to undo his belt then takes off his trousers.*

Now put them back on.

ALI *is taken aback but does not protest. He puts his trousers back on and tucks his shirt in. He fastens his belt and puts his shoes on. He finishes by tying his laces.*

Now take them off. *(Beat)* Take them off. Come on, you're holding everyone up.

ALI *takes his shoes off and removes his trousers again. He waits, holding them in his arms.*

Good man! Put them back on. *(Arabic)* Put your clothes back on, I said.

ALI *puts his trousers and shoes back on again. Then, just as he finishes tying his laces...*

Take them off.

ALI No!

DAVID *moves his gun closer to* ALI*'s head.*

DAVID Take off your trousers. Now. *(Arabic)* Yalla, yalla *[Come on, come on].*

ALI *complies and removes his trousers one more time.*

Now pick up your shoes. *(Beat)* Pick them up.

ALI *picks up his shoes and holds everything in a bundle in his arms.*

Now hop.

ALI What?

DAVID Hop. One leg—up and down—up and down. You understand? Do you think I enjoy standing here all day like this?

ALI *starts to hop up and down.*

Higher. Jump higher.

ALI *starts to hop as high as he can.* **DAVID** *moves away and continues to instruct the crowd where to go, ignoring* **ALI**, *who continues to hop.*

(Arabic) Everyone else! Move forward. Move forward. *(English)* Permits and ID cards. Hawiya. Hawiya.

After a moment **DAVID** *turns to* **ALI** *and gestures for him to go.*

Hey, my friend! Hey! You can go now!

ALI *stops hopping and starts to get dressed. He finishes and looks to* **DAVID**.

You want something?

ALI I hope it doesn't rain.

The sounds of turnstiles clanking. **ALI** *exits.*

Scene Ten

Interrogation room. ALI *is asleep in a chair.* DAHLIA *enters carrying her work bag and a paper grocery bag. She watches him for a few moments.*

DAHLIA Ali... Ali... Wake up...

ALI What? What's wrong?

Beat.

DAHLIA I have some good news. I've got you some support for your case.

ALI Support? What do you mean?

DAHLIA There's a prominent human right's lawyer called Nora Spiegler. She campaigns against the military occupation in the West Bank and she wants to help you.

ALI Why?

DAHLIA What do you mean, why?

ALI I have you. You're my lawyer.

DAHLIA You don't understand. She has represented Palestinians on some of the most high profile cases here. Even the courts are scared of her. Don't you see what she can do for you?

ALI But I want you to represent me.

DAHLIA Ali, I'm not going anywhere. I'm here. I've been in meetings with her all morning. I've passed on all your paperwork and she wants to represent you in court. She is going to try and push for your case to be dropped. She has promised me this.

ALI She can do that?

DAHLIA She is known for making cases fall apart by arguing that the occupation is illegal under international law. I have put everything in place. Just trust me with this.

Beat.

ALI I don't know what to say.

DAHLIA You'll be meeting her before your trial. It will be brief but she is aware of everything. I will be with you.

ALI Thank you.

DAHLIA I bought us some food to celebrate.

> DAHLIA *opens the bag and takes out some food, including some oranges.* ALI *takes an orange and stares at it.* DAHLIA *takes it off him, peels it, then halves it with him. They eat it together.*

ALI Why did we hide it for so long?

DAHLIA I was scared. We were young...

Beat.

ALI My God! Your father's face when I arrived... I saw your mother prompt him to close his mouth. I didn't know what to say? Do I say salaam—hello—shalom? I couldn't decide in time so I just held it, my hand outstretched, waiting for it to be taken.

DAHLIA Then my mother pulled you inside.

ALI She gave me a hug. She held me tightly. She said 'Welcome to our home.'

DAHLIA Because they wanted you there. And you could never accept that.

Beat.

ALI You had so many pictures in the hallway. Every year, another picture: Dahlia as a baby; Dahlia in nursery.

DAHLIA They told me how much they loved hearing your stories—

ALI Dahlia at school... The family on holiday—

DAHLIA They told me how charming you were. *(Hebrew. Imitating her mother)* 'He is adorable, Dahlia. He really is. *(English)* When will he visit again?'

ALI I was sat on your couch looking around at this home and I thought to myself, this is what a home feels like. Stable. Warm. Safe. And then... You had medals for valour hung up in your living room.

DAHLIA They adored you.

ALI You had this whole life that I never even knew about.

DAHLIA They wanted you to stay.

ALI I was sitting in your home and all I was thinking was who it belonged to?

DAHLIA What do you mean?

ALI Your parents' home. The house you felt safe growing up in. The house in which you learned to walk and talk. Who did it belong to?

DAHLIA It belongs to my parents.

ALI And before them?

DAHLIA It was my grandparents home.

ALI And who did your grandparents' buy it off?

DAHLIA How would I know that? I don't know who owned the house before my grandparents. They came over when the British were here.

ALI Because... I'm sitting on your couch... In your house... Your parents have welcomed me and I still haven't let you meet my father—

DAHLIA I told you I would wait—

ALI And all I am thinking of is... Who gave the British the right to give away our homes? *(Beat)* Why am I thinking this in your fucking home?

DAHLIA It's alright—

ALI You do all this for me and I'm thinking—

DAHLIA I did this because I wanted to make you happy. I wanted you to trust me. *(Beat)* In your house—in your old house—when I took you there. What did we see inside?

ALI Nothing!

DAHLIA Exactly. It was empty. No one lived there anymore. It was a sign. That's what you told me—

ALI I need to tell you this—

DAHLIA You don't.

ALI I had these thoughts. I had these thoughts of evicting you. In your... In your home!

DAHLIA It's alright. I understand. It's alright.

ALI It's not alright. I loved you and I am thinking—

DAHLIA I forced you to enter. I forced you to enter through a back door. No one was there. I had to pull you inside. What did we see when we entered?

ALI Boxes. Freshly sealed boxes with writing on them.

DAHLIA *To be removed! Ana's bedroom. Leah's bedroom. The kitchen.* Someone was moving out. They had taken everything but had left just a few boxes to be collected. *(Beat)* You sat me down on a single chair that was left behind and you went into the kitchen. You started cooking for me.

ALI *laughs, embarrassingly.*

You pretended you were cooking for me! You were chopping away at vegetables; frying meat; sprinkling spices. You brought out all these invisible dishes one at a time and insisted that I smell them.

ALI And then we ate together... How was my cooking?

DAHLIA Sublime. We must have been there for three hours. I told you we had to go to meet my parents but you insisted on what? What?

ALI Washing up.

DAHLIA Washing up, invisible fucking plates!

ALI My mother used to tell me a cook is not just defined by the amount of dishes coming out of the kitchen but also by the mess left behind.

DAHLIA I watched you as you pretended to wash every dish, every pan, cup, knife, and fork.

ALI And then you joined in. It wasn't just me, was it?

DAHLIA *kisses* ALI.

Pause.

DAHLIA I'm so sorry

ALI Don't be.

DAHLIA That shouldn't have happened.

ALI It did.

DAHLIA Shit!

ALI No one will know.

DAHLIA I should go.

ALI Dahlia—

DAHLIA I just wanted to let you know the good news. I've also organised some fresh clothes for you to wear on the day.

ALI Thank you.

DAHLIA It's just clothes.

ALI No. For Jaffa. You made it happen

*2008. We melt into the buffer zone between Gaza and
Israel.* ASHER *looks out. He is dressed in his military
garb.*

ASHER Guess what I'm looking at right now? The sea. *(Beat)*
And Gaza. I don't take my eyes off Gaza.

Beat.

There is a three-hundred metre buffer zone which surrounds
Gaza. No one enters it, this is the rule. Last week a bomb
was detonated and my partner was hit by the shrapnel.
The bomb was detonated over two-hundred metres away
and a shard of metal ripped through his jacket and entered
his shoulder.

Beat.

At two-hundred metres you will be injured by shrapnel.
Between one hundred and twenty, and sixty metres you could
lose a limb. Anything closer than sixty metres and you die.
You die. Welcome to my view. Welcome to the buffer zone.

2008. We transport to a beach. ASHER *is staring at* ALI
and DAHLIA *who are looking out into the sea.*

I found you.

DAHLIA Asher!

ASHER I'm sorry I'm late. I missed the celebrations! You didn't
even save me any food! Ima and aba told me you would be
down here.

DAHLIA This is / Ali—

ASHER You used to swim out as far as you could. Remember?
You would scare our parents like crazy.

DAHLIA Asher...

ASHER You were cruel. You made them think you had drowned!
(In Hebrew) What, I don't get a hug?

DAHLIA *walks up to* ASHER *and hugs him.*

DAHLIA This is—

ASHER They said you introduced your boyfriend to them.

ALI *(To Asher)* I don't want any trouble.

DAHLIA There isn't going to be any trouble.

ASHER *(Hebrew)* How long have you been keeping this from us?

DAHLIA *(Hebrew)* I am not going to explain myself to you.

ASHER *(Hebrew)* Is this why you didn't want to tell me?

ALI Dahlia, what's going on?

DAHLIA Nothing.

ASHER *(Hebrew)* I'm not leaving until you come back home with me.

DAHLIA Stop it. Stop it, Asher.

ALI What are you saying to her? What is he—

DAHLIA Nothing.

ASHER *(Hebrew)* I won't allow this, Dahlia. I won't allow this to happen to our family.

DAHLIA The family wanted him there. Fuck you.

ASHER The community will disown you. Think of our parents.

DAHLIA They wanted him there.

ASHER Think about how this makes us look! They see you bring an Arab into our home and they will never accept us again.

DAHLIA How dare you say this!

ASHER He deserves to hear it!

DAHLIA He has a name!

ASHER The neighbours have already been calling the house to ask who he is?

DAHLIA Fuck the neighbours! Come on, Ali. We're going.

ASHER I thought they were lying when they told me what you had done. Dahlia's boyfriend, they called him. And then I see ima cleaning up after an Arab! Cleaning the same plates and cutlery that we use on shabbat.

DAHLIA I'm going to kill you! *(Hebrew)* How can you say this in front of him? How can you do this to me? What did I ever do to you? They wanted him there! I wanted him there! If you don't like it then fuck off!

ASHER If you care for her, you'll go. Because she will never be accepted with you.

DAHLIA Don't talk to him, Ali.

ASHER Why are you here? Why are you really here?

DAHLIA Don't answer him.

ALI We love each other.

Beat.

ASHER She's Jewish. She's Jewish. We don't fit. You want us gone from here, remember?

ALI I love her!

ASHER You don't.

ALI I love her!

ASHER You don't understand what that means for us. For her.

ALI Let's go, Dahlia.

DAHLIA I'll never forgive you for this.

ASHER And you don't mind that she is a soldier?

DAHLIA Asher!

ASHER That she has spent two years stopping people like you entering Israel every fucking day.

DAHLIA Asher, stop!

ASHER You don't mind that she had to make sure your people don't try blowing themselves up on our buses or shoot rockets over our heads?

DAHLIA *pulls* ALI *away.*

ASHER Has she told you about her time in the Army? Have you told him, Dahlia?

ALI She has told me. She has told me everything.

DAHLIA Asher!

ASHER If you love him, surely he deserves to know.

DAHLIA *(Hebrew)* Asher, please, enough!

ASHER Dahlia is a hero. She saved a soldier from being killed. You must have noticed the medals in our home. She shot one of your martyrs. *(Beat)* It was a child. *(Beat)* You breed your children to hate us. You make us kill your children.

DAHLIA *slaps* ASHER.

ASHER You'll realise one day. I did this to save you. I did this because I love you.

ASHER *leaves. Silence.*

ALI Is it true?

DAHLIA I was going to tell you everything.

ALI What happened?

DAHLIA Ali, please don't—

ALI What happened?

Beat.

DAHLIA She was thirteen.

Beat.

She had to cross it to go to school and I remember she loved reading. I knew because she held a book under her arm every day, and every day I would ask her what she was reading but she would never reply back; wouldn't even make eye-contact with me. One week it was *Cinderella*, the next, *Kalilah wa Dimnah*; it went on and on. I realised she held her book so the soldiers wouldn't touch it when we searched her bag. Then one day I bought her a book and gave it to her. That was the first time she spoke. A shallow sound came out of her mouth. 'Thank you.' A few days later, I arrived late. I missed our daily ritual of silence, and me staring at her for a glimpse of the fantasy world she had her head stuck into. When I finally arrived at my post she was already there and had passed through. I saw her in the distance. She smiled at me. It was the first time I had seen her smile. I mean this glowing smile, that I could see clearly from about 200 feet away. She turned to go but then stopped. Then I saw her drop her bag to the ground and open it. I thought she would be putting her book inside but she pulled out a knife. She turned back towards the checkpoint and saw two soldiers with their backs towards her and she just ran towards them. I shouted at her to stop. I ran towards her. I just kept running and all the while shouting for her to stop. She was tiny and her feet hardly made a sound as she ran. I knew she would stab someone before I reached her... So I lifted up my gun, aimed at her legs and shot her. When I reached her she was still breathing but the bullet had gone through her abdomen. I ripped her shirt to put pressure on the puncture. She was still clutching her bag as papers were flying through the air—pictures, sketches, hand-written notes. Coloured pencils had spilled out of her pencil case and were scattered on the ground. There was a pool of blood around her head like a halo and her legs were spread apart with her tiny feet pointing in opposite directions and I realised she was already gone. And right there, peeping out of her bag was the book I had given her—*Alice in Wonderland*.

Silence.

ALI She was just a child.

DAHLIA She had a knife!

ALI She was a child who had been stopped and searched every day. *You* put that knife in her hands with your constant humiliation of her! Her crime was living in the wrong place.

DAHLIA She tried to attack a soldier.

ALI You killed a child, Dahlia!

DAHLIA I know what I did. I don't need you to remind me.

ALI When were you going to tell me?

DAHLIA After you met my family. I was scared of what you would do.

ALI How can I bring my father to meet you, knowing what you did?

DAHLIA Don't say that to me! Not after everything I have done.

ALI Like this? (**ALI** *takes out his permit*) Like this? (**ALI** *starts tearing up his permit*) Rubbish! Worthless!

DAHLIA Stop it! Ali, stop now—

ALI My permit? No! Your paper. Your ink. Your decisions, your fucking orders—

DAHLIA Ali! You need it! Stop, I said!

> **DAHLIA** *tries to stop him. He pushes her away.* **ALI** *throws the remnants at her.*

ALI There! It's yours. You can keep it.

DAHLIA Why are you doing this to me? I'm sorry, Ali.

ALI Tell her family. Not me. They're the ones you need forgiveness from.

> **ALI** *exits.*

Scene Eleven

ASHER *is staring out from a pillbox into Gaza. We hear* DAHLIA*'s personal voicemail followed by a beep.*

ASHER Dahlia. *(Beat)* It's me. This morning at five a.m., I saw a shepherd enter the buffer zone with sixty sheep. Sixty fucking sheep! Can you believe this? I'm thinking to myself, is he crazy? *(Beat)* I shouted to him: *(Arabic)* 'Hey, hey! Get out of there now! This is a military zone. Leave the area now!' *(English)* He ignores me, and you know what he did? He put up his middle finger and shouted something at me. My partner tells me it translated to: *My sheep need to graze. Stick your military zone and your gun up your arse.* He said that to me, Dahlia! *(Beat)* I hope that made you smile. *(Beat)* He continues to move towards me with these damn sheep. He is around two-hundred metres away from me now. *(Beat)* I followed protocol and proceeded to shoot a warning shot into the air. The sheep retreated a few metres but the shepherd shouted back at me. My partner says he was quite well versed in UN resolutions and quoted some to us. And you know what he did? You won't believe this. He holds his arms outstretched, shouting at me to shoot him. He told me to shoot him! I radio my commander to ask for assistance. He tells me to keep track of his distance. One-hundred and sixty metres. One-hundred and fifty metres. One-hunderd and forty metres. One-hundred and thirty metres. He tells me not to let him get any closer than one hundred metres. *(Beat)* I have the orders: shoot to kill. We cannot risk if one of his sheep has a bomb strapped to them. *(Beat)* He doesn't look a threat, Dahlia, rather just a pain in the arse. He is approaching one-hundred and ten metres now and my partner looks at me and says, 'what are you waiting for? Shoot him. Shoot him, now!' *(Beat)* But I can't. I'm scared. I'm scared to do anything. My partner grabs my gun from my hands and he aims. He shoots. *(Beat)* He shoots one of his sheep. The rest of the flock run back and the shepherd is left alone. 'Fuck Israel', he says. Then he heads back the

way he came. *(Beat)* Dahlia, talk to me, please. *(Beat)* All
that I said about Ali on the beach—

A steady beep, signalling the end of the recording.

Scene Twelve

DAHLIA *enters.* **ALI** *is waiting for her. He is smartly dressed in trousers and shirt.*

DAHLIA Good morning.

ALI Good morning. What do you think?

DAHLIA You look very handsome.

ALI I have a taxi waiting outside for the two of us. Table is booked for dinner at seven. Are you ready?

Beat.

DAHLIA How are you feeling?

ALI Scared.

DAHLIA You'll be fine. I'll come down with you to introduce you to Nora and then a car will take you to the courthouse.

ALI I feel you have done too much for me. I don't know how to repay you.

DAHLIA There is nothing to repay me for.

Beat.

ALI I have a favour to ask.

DAHLIA What?

ALI I've written a letter to my father. Can you deliver it for me?

DAHLIA Sure, I'll post it for you.

ALI No, I want you to give it to him, personally. Today if you can.

DAHLIA Ali, I've not met him.

ALI That's why I want you to give it to him.

ALI gives DAHLIA the letter. She puts it in her bag.

I told him you were writing a novel.

DAHLIA What?

ALI A novel. *(Beat)* With time, I stopped mentioning you and he never asked again. *(Beat)* I've been thinking a lot about my mother in here—what she would think of me... What she would think of you. I think she would have liked you.

DAHLIA walks towards ALI and kisses him. It's tender and for the first time we sense they could transcend these four prison walls.

DAHLIA I have something for you too.

DAHLIA produces a small box wrapped in cloth and holds it out for ALI.

ALI What is it?

ALI takes the box from DAHLIA and starts to open it.

DAHLIA Don't open it now. It's for after your trial. It's a surprise.

ALI I don't like surprises. *(Beat)* What's the first thing you want to do?

DAHLIA What?

ALI When I'm out. What's the first thing you want to do?

DAHLIA Can we talk about this after the trial—

ALI You know what I want? I want to go back to Jaffa beach with you. I want to spend the whole night there. I dreamt of this last night. Do you think that's possible?

DAHLIA Is that what you really want?

ALI Don't you?

Beat.

DAHLIA Yes. Yes, I do.

ALI You're not happy. I can see you are not happy with this.

DAHLIA I am happy.

ALI I'm scared I might not get the chance to say this again. I'm scared of—

DAHLIA You're going to get out of here.

ALI Why do I always believe everything you say? You have this way of making me feel like everything will work out.

DAHLIA Why are you telling me this?

ALI Because I want... I want you, Dahlia. I want you—fuck, I'm shaking. I'm shaking here — Leave with me.

DAHLIA What?

ALI You wanted that? I remember this, Dahlia—

DAHLIA That was a long time ago.

ALI Maybe. Is it a maybe, at least? I need to know, Dahlia, because I've put it all in that letter. Open it and read it now if you want proof. I've told my father I'm getting out of here. He knows there is nothing left in Bir Nabala. It's broken. But you and me, we could...we could start all over again.

DAHLIA Where would we go?

ALI We could travel.

DAHLIA Where would we go to?

ALI We could travel! *(Beat)* Switzerland.

DAHLIA Switzerland? Why Switzerland?

ALI Look, I'm thinking on the spot here, Dahlia. Bear with me, please.

DAHLIA My family are all here, Ali. And you want to go to Switzerland?

ALI Ok, maybe not Switzerland! Look, look, I'm stuck, Dahlia. I'm not moving forward here. I'm static. *(Beat)* Read the letter, I'm telling you the truth. *(Beat)* I love you. I know it's not the most romantic of settings. It's not on a beach, or by the sea. It's not staring out into the horizon—

DAHLIA Okay.

ALI I love you.

DAHLIA I said okay.

ALI Okay? Okay what?

DAHLIA Okay... I'll do it.

ALI Yes?

DAHLIA Yes.

ALI You mean it? Yes?

DAHLIA I've just said yes, haven't I?

Beat.

ALI You're a lawyer!

DAHLIA What?

ALI You can work as a lawyer anywhere in the world. I know you can do it. And me, I can get a job as working in...

DAHLIA Listen, when you are in the courtroom, they will ask you about the soldier. He's been found.

ALI How is he?

DAHLIA He's alive. He's been taken to hospital.

ALI Where did they find him?

DAHLIA On the outskirts of Bethlehem.

ALI Did they arrest anyone?

DAHLIA Five people. They're being questioned. Another was shot dead during the raid.

ALI What was their name?

DAHLIA This is good news. They will ask you what you saw that night. You just tell them what you told me.

ALI I will. (*Beat*) An American goes missing during the opening of the US embassy and we all get rounded up.

Pause.

DAHLIA How did you know he was an American?

ALI What?

DAHLIA How did you know the soldier was a settler who had come over from America?

ALI What are you talking about? Everyone knows he was American.

DAHLIA Who? (*Beat*) No one knows, Ali. No one knows because he *is* an American. Because an American born soldier was kidnapped on the day of the opening of the US embassy.

ALI You must have told me.

DAHLIA I didn't. I never told you. How did you know, Ali?

ALI I don't know. I don't know. This is ridiculous—

DAHLIA You know who took him, don't you?

ALI What? No. No. How can you ask me this?

DAHLIA Is that why you wanted to know who was shot when they found him? You know them, don't you? You know who did this!

ALI Rubbish. How would I know this? I was arrested! I've been in here with you!

DAHLIA I don't believe you. Tell me the truth.

ALI I told you the truth! They found him! They got him back! Tell them to ask him.

DAHLIA How did you know he was an American settler? You need to tell me what happened before you leave here.

Beat.

ALI Nothing happened. I fucking heard about him. Chatter. Chatter. This is all I heard.

DAHLIA You're not leaving here until you tell me the truth, Ali. No more lies. Tell me.

ALI You abandoned me. You lied to me. Who is this Nora? You are my lawyer and you abandoned me!

Beat.

DAHLIA I'm not a lawyer. I have never been a lawyer. Now tell me what happened?

ALI What's going on, Dahlia?

Pause.

DAHLIA I work in intelligence.

ALI OK, now you are joking. You? Intelligence? Like what? Shin Bet?

Silence. **ALI** *realises* **DAHLIA** *is not lying anymore.*

Dahlia, don't do this to me! Please. Please.

ALI *prowls around the room, unsure what to do.*

They sent you because they know about us, don't they?

DAHLIA I never knew I would see you in here. I'm telling you the truth. But I need you to tell me what happened. What did you see that night? *(Beat)* I vouched for you, Ali. When you lied about your name, I vouched for you. Do you know how difficult that was! When they asked me what you knew, I told them nothing. *(Beat)* I could be sent to prison for this!

ALI *(indicates his clothes)* Is this why I got these? Special treatment! You made me believe you could get me out of here!

There is a knock at the door.

DAHLIA *(Hebrew)* Hello?

PRISON GUARD *(Hebrew)* You have a visitor who has arrived. She is waiting outside for you. Her name is Ms Nora Spiegler.

DAHLIA *(Hebrew)* We'll be out in a moment. *(In English)* She's here.

ALI And who is she? Mossad?

DAHLIA No. I meant it.

ALI Am I supposed to thank you?

DAHLIA No. I'm not asking for any gratitude.

ALI Is it common practice to kiss your fucking suspects. *(Beat)* I was a suspect, wasn't I?

DAHLIA Every Palestinian within the vicinity of the soldier's last known whereabouts was rounded up and has been questioned. You were just one of them.

ALI Do you know what would happen if anyone found out I have talked to an intelligence officer. They would think I am an informant. They would destroy me. *(Beat)* I told you I wanted to leave here with you. You said yes. What were you going to do? Organise a private jet out of here, all paid for by the Israeli Secret Service? *(Silence)* You know, without their uniform, they look just like us. *(Beat)* We grabbed him before he could reach for his gun. We overpowered him; wrestling him to the ground. You don't think, you just let instinct instruct you... We were lost and so was he.

DAHLIA What did you do to him?

ALI I dragged him into a secluded area. He was screaming, kicking, asking for help. Begging me. Begging me, for forgiveness. He had an American accent. He was screaming— screaming that he was an American and was living in the settlement of Kedumin. He must have thought we would have mercy on a foreigner. But not today.

DAHLIA What did you do, Ali?

ALI We stripped him of his weapons. We told him, we told him, we are equal now. I took his military jacket off. And do you know what I did? I put it on. I wore it like it was a fucking souvenir and paraded around in it while everyone cheered for me. *(Beat)* He was crying. Crying to be freed for his family's sake. I told him to shut up but he kept screaming about his family. Crying for his family. *(Beat)* So I hit him. Once. I hit him as hard as I could. To stop his sounds. It hurts, hitting someone, bone on bone, it hurts you too. I kept hitting him over and over again until the skin around my fist split open. I could see blood crawling down my hand. His blood and mine, mixed together. Something broke. I could hear it. Jaw, nose—something cracked. He held onto me as if we were embracing. Our heads were locked together as I held him up. And he just held onto me. He didn't let go. At the moment when his eyes started to close, I released him. Everyone looked at me, but they were silent. And all I could think, was what my mother would think of me right now. He was dragged away. I never saw him again after that.

Silence. **ALI** *approaches* **DAHLIA**.

DAHLIA Don't come near me. Stay away from me.

ALI Dahlia—

A knock at the door.

PRISON GUARD *(Hebrew)* Hey! I don't have all day. Are you coming out or not?

Beat.

ALI What are you going to do?

DAHLIA You need to go.

ALI Tell me, please...

DAHLIA I don't know... I don't know... Please leave now.

ALI *goes to leave. Before he exits, he sees the package that* **DAHLIA** *brought for him. He picks it up and unwraps* *it. He reveals a small box. He opens it and looks inside, without the audience seeing what it contains.* **ALI** *closes the box and holds it out for* **DAHLIA** *to take back.* **DAHLIA** *walks up to him and takes the box.*

The door opens. An officer lurks in the shadows of the door. **ALI** *exits.* **DAHLIA** *remains alone on stage, holding the box. Blackout.*

Scene Thirteen

2002. West Bank wall. We find young ALI *and* DAHLIA, *14 years old, occupying their meeting place.*

ALI I had a dream last night. There was no Israel or Palestine.

DAHLIA Well, that's a stupid dream.

ALI There was no wall, no soldiers, no tanks, no suicide bombings, and no guns. There were no roadblocks, no checkpoints, and no evictions. There was just you and me, and we were travelling on a bus to Jaffa.

DAHLIA What happened when we got there?

ALI The sky was a pure soft blue, and the air crisp and clear when we breathed it in. And there it was. Our house. It was untouched and stood tall, strong, and beautiful, and it looked like it could survive a century of war. We crossed the orange grove, picking one each as we passed.

DAHLIA Who else was there?

ALI No one. It was just you and me.

DAHLIA It sounds amazing. Can we go there one day?

ALI *reveals the same small box that* DAHLIA *gave to him in Scene Twelve. He hands it to* DAHLIA. *She opens it to reveal a vintage door key.*

ALI This is the key to my home. My grandfather gave it to my father and he gave it to me. One day, we will go back there.

ALI *gives* DAHLIA *the key. She inspects it.*

DAHLIA It looks so old. How do you know if it still works?

ALI Because it worked in my dream. *(Beat)* I want you to have it.

DAHLIA I can't take it. It's yours.

ALI You can give it back to me when we get there. If the soldiers find it on me *now*, they'll take it away. You can keep it safe for us.

DAHLIA What about the wall? How will you cross once it's finished?

ALI I'll dig a tunnel.

DAHLIA A tunnel?

ALI A tunnel to take us all the way to Jaffa.

DAHLIA Are you crazy?

ALI *(proud)* Maybe I am!

DAHLIA A tunnel that long will take a lifetime to dig.

ALI Well, I am fourteen now. We probably won't be able to get married until we're at least thirty? So, I think that gives me more than enough time. *(Beat)* We don't *have* to get married. But you know, it's good to have a plan in life, my father says.

Beat.

DAHLIA That sounds like a good plan to me.

Beat.

ALI Deal?

DAHLIA Deal.

The two shake hands securing the deal. The sounds of gunfire rattle in the distance; young **ALI** *and* **DAHLIA** *completely oblivious to it all.*

Blackout.

PROPS

Three chairs
Binoculars for Gaza scene
Bags for children
Box and key
Camera phone
Dates to break fast
Files for Dahlia, including pictures of suspects
Letter to Ali's father
Metal bowl
Oranges
Ali's ID card
Israeli permit
Picnic food
Pictures of Jaffa
Sandwich
Slingshot
Takeaway meal
Water

VISIT THE SAMUEL FRENCH BOOKSHOP AT THE ROYAL COURT THEATRE

Browse plays and theatre books, get expert advice and enjoy a coffee

Samuel French Bookshop
Royal Court Theatre
Sloane Square
London
SW1W 8AS
020 7565 5024

Shop from thousands of titles on our website

 samuelfrench.co.uk

 samuelfrenchltd

 samuel french uk

9 780573 116391